DIRECTORY
OF AMERICAN
POETRY BOOKS

DIRECTORY
OF AMERICAN
POETRY BOOKS

Edited by Poets House

Compiled through the Poetry Publication Showcase

ASPHODEL PRESS

Moyer Bell

Wakefield, Rhode Island & London

127845

Published by Asphodel Press

First Edition

LIBRARY OF CONGRESS
CATALOGING-IN-PUBLICATION DATA

Directory of American poetry books/
[edited by] Poets House.—1st ed.

p.   cm.
Includes indexes.

1. American poetry—Bibliography. 2. Literature
publishing—United States—Directories. I. Poets
House (Firm)
Z1231.P7D57 1993
[PS303]   93-17778
016.811008—dc20   CIP
ISBN 1-55921-099-0 (pb.)

Printed in the United States of America.
Distributed in North America by Publishers Group
West, P. O. Box 8843, Emeryville CA 94662,
800-788-3123 (in California 510-658-3453).

ACKNOWLEDGMENTS

We would like to express our appreciation to the Poets House Board of Directors, especially President Emeritus, Stanley Kunitz, and President, Margo Viscusi, for their advice and support for the Poetry Publication Showcase and this *Directory;* and to the Poets House Poets Advisory Committee, especially Jonathan Galassi and Dan Halpern. We would also like to thank the many people whose advice helped shape both projects: among them, Jill Bialosky, Bea Gates, Jewelle Gomez, Herbert Leibowitz, Harvey Shapiro, Barbara Smith, and Eliot Weinberger.

We are grateful to The Greenwall Foundation, The Andrew W. Mellon Foundation, the National Endowment for the Arts, and the Witter-Bynner Foundation for Poetry for funding that launched the Poetry Publication Showcase.

We thank all those who volunteered their time and expertise to the project, especially Marianne Burke, Anne-Marie Levine, Michael Morse, Esther Trepal, and William Winfield.

INTRODUCTION

This *Directory*—the first of its kind—is a buyer's guide for poetry readers, a publishing guide for poets, and a map of the current status of poetry publishing in America. It reflects the entire range of poetry book publishing, during the course of a one-year period, by large and small publishers across the country, including commercial, university, and independent presses. It provides all of the information needed to purchase (either wholesale or retail) any book listed.

The *Directory of American Poetry Books* grows out of the Poets House Poetry Publication Showcase, an annual celebration of new poetry releases inaugurated at Poets House in New York City in June, 1992. Conceived and founded by Executive Director Lee Briccetti, the Poetry Publication Showcase is a series of events that includes panel discussions, receptions, and readings, all presented within the context of an exhibit of the year's new poetry releases. The exhibit— almost 1000 books from some 300 publishers in 1992 alone— demonstrates the diversity and range of poetic voices in the United States.

This first edition of the *Directory* is based on the Exhibit Catalog compiled to accompany the 1992 Showcase. After the events were over and the exhibit came down, requests for copies of the catalog kept pouring in. Obviously, the catalog was fulfilling a need. We are delighted that now, through Asphodel Press and the generosity of The

Andrew W. Mellon Foundation, the catalog has been reconfigured as a directory.

Future editions, to be published annually, will be cumulative. Beginning with the second edition, short descriptions of each book will be included, and the *Directory* will be organized by author. Eventually, it will become the closest thing we have to a "Poetry Books in Print."

The Poetry Publication Showcase is about poetry now, poetry this year. More, it is about poetry within the economic and cultural context of our times. The exhibit explores the interdependence of poet and publisher in bringing poetry to the public. Showcase panel discussions bring together poets, publishers, booksellers, reviewers, and others on whom the enterprise of poetry depends. Providing an opportunity for a celebration of poetry on a broad scale, the Showcase also provides audiences and participants the opportunity to achieve a more comprehensive view of poetry in our society.

During the course of planning and assembling the Showcase, we soon realized that poetry is significantly under-represented in standard bibliographic sources. Many of the books exhibited would not be included in *Books in Print*, many would not be reviewed, many of the reviews that *did* get written would not be indexed in *The Reader's Guide to Periodical Literature*.

Conversations with publishers from all over the country revealed that poetry—and poetry readers—suffer from the inadequate marketing and distribution of poetry books. While the publicity departments of large commercial publishers sent us their new poetry books for exhibit in a matter-of-course manner, publishers of smaller presses, who often cannot afford to participate in national and international book fairs, greeted our invitation to exhibit with great eagerness. No wonder: The panel discussing "Selling Poetry: Sales and Public Access" considered dolefully the fact that only about 400 bookstores nationwide stock and sell any amount of poetry regularly. Convinced there is no market for poetry, bookstores hesitate to order it, distributors to market it, editors to assign it for review. Lack of marketing and distribution mechanisms impacts negatively on both the supply and the demand sides of a marketplace equation, effectively suppressing the visibility of poetry in our society.

Often, poets are resistant to considering the commercial side of poetry publishing and distribution. But again and again, Showcase panel discussions led to the same conclusion: Those who care about poetry must learn how the market functions in order to act as informed advocates for the art.

This *Directory* is our response to these issues. Our rule in compiling it was inclusiveness rather than selection. This is not the best of American poetry. It is not all of American poetry. But it is— to the best of our ability to make it so—a significant sample of American poetry published during this one year. While the Showcase Exhibit will continue to represent only the newest poetry books published, the goal of the *Directory of American Poetry Books* is to list all poetry in print. Look for future editions: Each one will bring us closer to that goal.

Using the *Directory of American Poetry Books*

For each publisher included in the *Directory*, we provide an address, the name of a contact person at the press, and a telephone number. Distributors or wholesalers that carry the books and special instructions for ordering them follow.

For each book we give the author, title, price, number of pages, ISBN, and publication date. If both paper and hardcover are available, both are described. Where only one price appears, assume that it is for a paperback copy. A complete index of authors begins on page 105. An index of titles begins on page 133.

Many bookstores that participate in STOP (Single Title Order Plan) will be happy to place special orders for you for any of the books.

Most poetry publishers will be happy to fill individual orders directly. Most will also be happy to send you a full catalog of their titles. When ordering by mail, please be aware that shipping and handling charges are not included in the listing and that most poetry publishers can only fill prepaid orders.

Poets and readers, demonstrate your demand for poetry! Broadening public access to the art of poetry is a responsibility we all share. The marketplace is ruled by the law of supply and demand. Write poetry, publish it, yes, but review it too, increasing its visibility. Write to your newspapers and magazines to let them know you would like to read more poetry reviews in their pages. Demonstrate your demand for poetry publicly by ordering poetry books through your local bookseller and by asking for them at your public library.

Booksellers, librarians, demonstrate the supply! The range of poetry included in the following pages suggests that there is no one aesthetic, or culture, no one age group, or personality type, or socio-economic background that finds poetry interesting. Like the kiwi fruit, if it is sold everywhere, it will be tasted. If it is tasted, anything can happen. By planning and producing the Showcase, we at Poets House learned that poetry is limited by the framework within which it exists, and that changing that framework depends on all of us.

—Jane Preston
Project Coordinator
Poetry Publication Showcase

Poets House is a *place for poetry*—a library and meeting place that invites poets and the public to step into the living tradition of poetry. Founded in 1985 by Stanley Kunitz and the late Elizabeth Kray, Poets House offers resources, literary events, and education programs that document the wealth and diversity of poetry and stimulate public dialog on issues of poetry in culture.

DIRECTORY OF AMERICAN POETRY BOOKS

A

Adams Press
6975 South Dearborn Street
Terre Haute, Indiana 47802
Imad Shouery
*To order: Contact Indiana State
University Bookstore,
550 Chestnut Street, #102,
P. O. Box 9027, Terra Haute,
Indiana 47808, Attention:
Janice Marsh*

Imad Shouery
Songs from Hellas
$6.95 52 pages Spring 1991
Yassimine and Thorny Roses
$7.95 72 pages May 1992

Africa World Press
P.O. Box 1892
Trenton, New Jersey 08607
Kassahan Checole, Publisher
(609) 771-1666
Distributed by The Red Sea Press

Rashidah Ismaili
*Missing in Action and
Presumed Dead*
$24.95, Cloth, 0-86543-296-1
$9.95, Paper, 0-86543-297-X
111 pages Fall 1992

**Ahsahta Press at
Boise State University**
Department of English
Boise, Idaho 83725
Dale K. Boyer, Co-editor
Orvis Burmaster; Tom Trusky
(208) 385-1999
Distributed by: SPD; Truck
*To order: Contact Bookstore,
BSU, 1910 University Drive,
Boise, Idaho 83725
(205) 385-1432*

Ken McCullough
Sycamore-Oriole
$6.95 64 pages
0-916272-50-8 November 1991

Gerrye Payne
The Year-God
$6.95 62 pages
0-916272-51-6 March 1992

alicejamesbooks
33 Richdale Avenue
Cambridge, Mass 02140
(617) 354-1408

Jeffrey Greene
To the Left of the Worshiper
$9.95 72 pages
0-914086-93-6 October 1991

Nancy Lagomarsino
The Secretary Parables
$9.95 72 pages
0-914086-92-8 September 1991

Cheryl Savageau
Home Country
$9.95 72 pages
0-914086-94-4 March 1992

Jean Valentine
The River at Wolf
$9.95 72 pages
0-914086-95-2 May 1992

Alileah Press
One University Place
New York, New York 10003
Alison Alpert, Publisher
(212) 777-0163

David Shaddock
In This Place Where
SOMETHING'S MISSING Lives
$21.00 40 pages
0-9627875-0-7 1992

Alleluia Press
P.O. Box 103
Allendale, New Jersey 07401
(201) 327-3513
(201) 327-4947 FAX

Catherine de Vinck
Poems of the Hidden Way
$9.75 142 pages
0-911726-53-5 January 1992

American Literary Press
11419 Cronridge Drive #10
Owings Mills, Maryland 21117
Alisa M. Hoffman, Senior Editor
(410) 356-2000

Gloria J. Childs
No Problimos
$8.50 48 pages
1-56167-085-5 April 1992

A. L. Danner
In the Verse Way: One Black
American's Perspective
$10.00 80 pages
1-56167-083-9 April 1992

Donna Dickey Guyer
Clippings
$15.00, Cloth 149 pages
1-56167-071-5 February 1992

Loverta Holloway
"Reflections" A Journey of Love
$9.95 64 pages
1-56167-074-X January 1992

Marsha Deborah Khoury
A Pledge to an Enchanted Dream
$6.95 32 pages
1-56167-075-8 February 1992

Robert Lenthart
Auburn Dreams
$5.95 32 pages
1-56167-014-6 March 1992

Liz Mendez
Hologram of Love
$6.95 64 pages
1-56167-066-9 January 1992

Teresa Diane Phillips
Love: Passion and Pain
$8.95 64 pages
1-56167-076-6 February 1992

Steven A. Seager
Thirteenth at Love's Table
$5.95 64 pages
1-56167-081-2 April 1992

Chrisoula Simos
*Inner Landscapes Outer
Realms*
$12.95 64 pages
1-56167-078-2 April 1992

Amethyst Press
c/o Inland Book Company
P.O. Box 120261
East Haven, CT 06512
(203) 467-4257

Tim Dlugos
Strong Place
$9.95 128 pages
0-927200-13-9 June 1992

Amherst Writers & Artists Press
Box 1076, Amherst, MA 01004
Pat Schneider
(413) 253-3307

Doug Anderson
Bamboo Bridge
$8.00 33 pages
0-941895-07-6 Fall 1991

Margaret Robison
Red Creek: A Requiem
$9.00 50 pages
0-941895-08-4 January 1992

Ampersand Press
Roger Williams University
Creative Writing Program
Bristol, Rhode Island 02809
Martha Christina, Director
(401) 254-3217
Distributed by: SPD; Inland

Brendan Galvin
*Outer Life: The Poetry of
Brendan Galvin*
Edited by Martha Christina
$10.00 190 pages
0-935331-12-3 December 1991

Ancient Mariners Press
229 North Fountain
Wichita, Kansas 67208
James Mechem

Gina Bergamino
Open Season
$2.00 24 pages March 1992
Oma's Story
$2.00 20 pages August 1991

Harriet Zinnes
Book of Twenty
$2.00 24 pages March 1992

Arjuna Library Press
1025 Garner Street, D, #18
Colorado Springs
Colorado 80905-1774
Joseph A. Uphoff, Jr., Director

Joseph A. Uphoff, Jr.
The Ghost Papers
$3.00 44 pages
0-943123-18-6 October 1991
The Poet's Universe
$7.00 130 pages
0-943123-20-8 1992

Arte Publico Press
University of Houston
Houston, Texas 77204
Marina Trisan, Assistant
Director; Nicolas Kanellos,
Publisher (713) 743-2841
Distributed by: Baker & Taylor;
Bookpeople; Ingram; Inland

Lorna Dee Cervantes
*From the Cables of Genocide:
Poems on Love and Hunger*
$7.00 78 pages
1-55885-033-3 Fall 1991

Pat Mora
Communion
$7.00 92 pages
1-55885-035-X Fall 1991

Artifact Press, Ltd.
900 Tanglewood Drive
Concord, Mass 01742-4947
Connie Hershey
(508) 369-8933
(508) 371-7523 FAX
Distributed by: Baker & Taylor;
Bookpeople; Inland

*Truth and Lies That Press for
Life: 60 Los Angeles Poets*
Edited by Connie Hershey
$12.95 215 pages
0-9629097-0-X 1991

The Ashland Poetry Press
Ashland University
Ashland, Ohio 44805
Robert McGovern; Nancy Grimm
(419) 289-5118

William Sylvester
Heavy Metal from Pliny
$2.00 10 pages
0-912592-32-X March 1992

Ashod Press
138-40 64th Avenue
Flushing, New York 11367-1110
Jack Antreassian
(718) 762-8182

Leonardo Alishan
Dancing Barefoot on Broken Glass
$7.50 77 pages
0-935102-29-9 Fall 1991

Vahan Derian
Coming to Terms: Selected Poems
Translated by Diana Der Hovanessian
$7.50 77 pages
0-935102-30-2 Fall 1991

Asphodel Press/Moyer Bell
Kymbolde Way
Wakefield, Rhode Island 02879
Jennifer Moyer, Co-publisher
(401) 789-0074
(401) 789-3793 FAX
Distributed by Publishers Group West

William Bronk
Some Words
$9.95 72 pages
1-55921-023-0 October 1992

Constance Hunting
The Myth of Horizon
$12.95 176 pages
1-55921-044-3 May 1991

Asylum Arts
P.O. Box 6203
Santa Maria, California 93456
Greg Boyd, Publisher
(805) 928-8774
Distributed by Inland/InBook

Charles Baudelaire
Echoes of Baudelaire: Selected Poems
Bilingual edition. Translated from French by Kendall Lappin
$17.95, Cloth, 0-878580-28-0
$9.95, Paper, 0-878580-27-2
208 pages March 1992

Edouard Roditi
Choose Your Own World
$20.00, Cloth, 1-878580-40-X
$7.95, Paper 1-878580-39-6
111 pages March 1992

Gallic Echoes: A Selection of Poems
Bilingual edition. Translated from French by Kendall Lappin
$16.95, Cloth, 0-878580-26-4
$8.95, Paper, 0-878580-25-6
152 pages September 1991

B

The Bank Street Press
24 Bank Street
New York, New York 10014
Mary Bertschmann
(212) 255-0692

Mary York Sampson
52 Sonnets
$10.00 64 pages
0-935505-07-5 October 1991

William L. Bauhan, Publisher
P.O. Box 443
Dublin, New Hampshire 03444
John S. Tarner
(603) 563-8020

Jane Baldwin Gillespie
Cloud Shadows
$8.95 79 pages
0-87233-101-6 1992

Sarah Singer
The Gathering
$8.95 80 pages
0-87233-102-4 1992

Belhue Press
2501 Palisade Avenue, #A1
Riverdale, Bronx, NY 10463
Tom Caine, Perry Brass, Editors
(718) 884-6606; phone or FAX
Distributed by: Inland;
Bookpeople; Alamo Square
Distributors

Perry Brass
Sex-charge
$6.95 76 pages
0-9627123-0-2 1991

Bilingual Press
Arizona State University
Hispanic Research Center
Box 872702
Tempe, Arizona 85287-2702
Karen Van Hooft, Managing
Editor; Ann Waggoner Aken,
Associate Editor,
(602) 965-3867

Ricardo Pau-Llosa
Bread of the Imagined
$7.00 88 pages
0-927534-16-9 May 1992

Birch Brook Press
P.O. Box 81
Delhi, New York 13753
Tom Tolnay, Publisher
(212) 353-3326

Barbara de la Cuesta
If There Weren't So Many of
Them You Might Say They
Were Beautiful
$12.00 64 pages
0-913559-17-2 Spring 1992

Black Sparrow Press
24 Tenth Street
Santa Rosa, California 95401
Michele Filshie, Asst. Publisher
(707) 579-4011

Charles Bukowski
The Last Night of the Earth Poems
$25.00, Cloth, 0-87685-864-7
$15.00, Paper, 0-87685-863-9
405 pages March 1992

Tom Clark
Sleepwalker's Fate: New &
Selected Poems 1965-1991
$25.00, Cloth, 0-87685-870-1
$12.50, Paper, 0-87685-869-8
212 pages May 1992

Joanne Kyger
Just Space: Poems 1979-1989
$20.00, Cloth, 0-87685-835-3
$12.50, Paper, 0-87685-834-5
142 pages September 1991

D. H. Lawrence
Birds, Beasts and Flowers!
$20.00, Cloth, 0-87685-867-1
$12.50, Paper, 0-87685-866-3
213 pages May 1992

Gerard Malanga
Three Diamonds
$20.00, Cloth, 0-87685-838-8
$12.50, Paper, 0-87685-837-X
216 pages September 1991

Black Thistle Press
491 Broadway
New York, New York 10012
Hollis Melton, President
(212) 219-1898
(212) 477-2714 FAX
Distributed by Inland

Vyt Bakaitis
City Country
$11.95 146 pages
0-9628181-2-7 1991

Black Tie Press
Box 440004
Houston, Texas 77244
Peter Gravis
(713) 789-5119

Harry Burrus
The Jaguar Portfolio
$12.50 126 pages
0-941749-25-8 Fall 1991

Craig Cotter
*There's Something Seriously
Wrong With Me*
$10.50 64 pages
0-941749-27-4 Fall 1991

Sekou J. Karanja
Waiting for the Rain
$7.95 64 pages
0-941749-26-6 Fall 1991

Toni Ortner
Requiem
$6.95 48 pages
0-941749-22-3 Fall 1991

Donald Rawley
Malibu Stories
$12.50 68 pages
0-941749-23-1 Fall 1991
Mecca
$12.50 108 pages
0-941749-24-X Fall 1991

Dieter Weslowski
Candles of Wheat
$6.95 48 pages
0-941749-19-3 Fall 1991

Steve Wilson
Allegory Dance
$10.50 64 pages
0-941749-28-2 Fall 1991

Blue Heron Press
P.O. Box 550
Thibodaux, Louisiana 70302
Carolyn Portier Gorman,
Publisher
(504) 446-8201

John Finlay
A Prayer to the Father
Edited by David Middleton
$8.00 36 pages
0-9621724-7-2 March 1992

A Garland for John Finlay
Edited by David Middleton
$6.00 32 pages
0-9621724-6-4 October 1991

BOA Editions
92 Park Avenue
Brockport, New York 14420
A. Poulin, Jr., President
(716) 473-1896

Charles Baudelaire
The Flowers of Evil and
Paris Spleen
Bilingual edition. Translated
by William H. Crosby
$15.00 489 pages
0-918526-87-6 1991

Lucille Clifton
Quilting: Poems 1987-1990
89 pages
0-918526-81-7 1991

Arthur Rimbaud
A Season in Hell &
Illuminations
Bilingual edition. Translated
by Bertrand Mathieu
$12.50 176 pages
0-918526-89-2 1991

Bogg Publications
422 North Cleveland Street
Arlington, Virginia 22201
John Elsberg, Publisher
(703) 243-6019

Derrick Buttress
It Is You We Are Trying to Love
free for postage
20 pages September 1991

Sheila Martindale
There Is a Place
free for postage
20 pages March 1992

Bosck Publishing House
P.O. Box 2311
Los Angeles, California
90051-0311
Kenya G. Williams, Sales
(213) 750-3413
Distributed by Baker & Taylor

Beatrice Garrett
A Bite of Black History
$14.95, Cloth, 0-9629887-1-5
$9.95, Paper, 0-99629887-0-7
58 pages January 1992

Bottom Dog Press
c/o Firelands College
Huron, Ohio 44839
Larry Smith, Editor/Publisher
(419) 433-5560
Distributed by: Baker & Taylor;
Borders Inc.; Midwest Library
Service

Jeff Gundy
Inquiries
$5.95 59 pages
0-933087-22-5 1992

Kenneth Patchen
Awash With Roses: The
Collected Love Poems of
Kenneth Patchen
Edited by Larry Smith and Laura
Smith
$19.95, Cloth, 0-933087-19-5
$9.95, Paper, 0-933087-21-7
176 pages October 1991

Bottom Fish Press
P.O. Box 82, Ingraham Hill Road
Binghamton, New York 13903
Thomas Haines
(607) 723-3926

Richard Martin
White Man Appears on
Southern California Beach
$9.95 71 pages
0-9627420-0-7 1991

Boyds Mills Press
910 Church Street
Honesdale, Pennsylvania 18431
Pamela F. Sader, Publisher's
Assistant
(717) 253-0179
Distributed by St. Martin's Press

Brod Bagert
Let Me Be...the Boss: Poems
for Kids to Perform
$14.95, Cloth
1-56397-099-6 June 1992

John Ciardi
The Monster Den
$13.95, Cloth 64 pages
1-878093-35-5 October 1991
You Know Who
$13.95, Cloth 64 pages
1-878093-34-7 October 1991

Georgia Heard
Creatures of Earth, Sea and Sky
$15.95, Cloth 32 pages
1-56397-013-9 March 1992

William Jay Smith
Big and Little
$15.95, Cloth 32 pages
1-56397-023-6 March 1992

Street Rhymes Around the World
Edited by Jane Yolen
$16.95, Cloth 40 pages
1-878093-53-3 March 1992

Behind the King's Kitchen:
A Roster of Rhyming Riddles
Compiled by William Jay Smith
and Carol Ra
$18.95, Cloth 48 pages
1-56397-024-4 March 1992

George Braziller
60 Madison Avenue
New York, New York 10010
Jeff Turrentine
(212) 889-0909

The Thirty-six Immortal
Women Poets: A Poetry Album
Illusustrated by Chobunsai
Eishi. Translated by Andrew
J. Pekarik
$45.00, Cloth, 0-8076-1256-1
$24.95, Paper, 0-8076-1257-X
192 pages 1991

Broadside Press
P.O. Box 04257
Detroit, Michigan 48204
Hilda Vest, Editor/Publisher
Don Vest, Business Manager
(313) 934-1231

Murray Jackson
*Watermelon Rinds and
Cherry Pits*
$7.00 88 pages
0-940713-04-7 1991

Sharon Smith-Knight
*Wine Sip and Other
Delicious Poems*
$7.00 78 pages
0-940713-06-3 1991

Broken Moon Press
P.O. Box 24585
Seattle, Washington 98124-0585
Paula Ladenburg
(206) 548-1340
Distributed by InBook

Julian Beck
living in volkswagen buses
$12.95 144 pages
0-913089-24-9 Spring 1992

Anita Endrezze
at the helm of twilight
$12.95 144 pages
0-913089-26-5 April 1992

Peter Levitt
Bright Root, Dark Root
$12.95 113 pages
0-913089-20-6 Fall 1991
One-Hundred Butterflies
$10.95 110 pages
0-913089-27-3 April 1992

**Brunswick Publishing
Corporation**
Route 1, Box 1A1
P.O. Box 555
Lawrenceville, Virginia 23868
Marianne Salzmann
(804) 848-3865

Richard Bondira
Tales the Wind Told Me
$8.95 68 pages
1-55618-097-7 Fall 1991

W. C. Lane
*The Passing Thought of a
Country Man*
$16.95 110 pages
1-55618-107-8 Fall 1991

Connell Linson
*Images/Glimpses and Other
Sightings*
$8.95 60 pages
1-55618-111-6 April 1992

John J. Soldo
In The Indies
$9.95 68 pages
1-55618-089-6 Fall 1991

Burning Deck
71 Elmgrove
Providence, Rhode Island 02906
Rosmarie Waldrop, Co-editor
(401) 351-0015
Distributed by SPD

Walter Abish
99: The New Meaning
$20.00, Cloth, 0-930901-67-3
$8.00, Paper, 0-930901-66-5
112 pages Fall 1991

Lew Daly
*E. Dickinson on a Sleepwalk
with the Alphabet Prowling
Around Her*
$4.00 24 pages
0-930901-69-X

Tina Darragh
Striking Resemblance
$7.00 64 pages
0-930901-64-9 Fall 1991

Forrest Gander
Eggplants and Lotus Root
$5.00 36 pages
0-930901-78-9 1991

Barbara Guest
The Countess from Minneapolis
$8.00 52 pages
0-930900-06-5 1991

John Hawkes
Island Fire
$5.00 12 pages
0-930901-59-2 1991

Julie Kalendek
The Fundamental Difference
$5.00 40 pages
0-930901-79-7 1991

Tom Mandel
Realism
$8.00 80 pages
0-930901-70-3 1991

Harry Mathews
Out of Bounds
$5.00 28 pages
0-930901-61-4 1991

Gale Nelson
Stare Decisis
$9.00 142 pages
0-930901-72-X Fall 1991

Jena Osman
Twelve Parts of Her
$4.00 24 pages
0-930901-63-01991

Stephen Rodefer
Passing Duration
$8.00 64 pages
0-930901-76-2 1991

Marjorie Welish
The Windows Flew Open
$8.00 80 pages
0-930901-74-6 1991

C

C & D Publishing
1017 SW Morrison #500
Portland, Oregon 97205
Craig McPherson; Dick Friedrich
(503) 274-8780

Susan Pakenen Holway
*Remember Where You
Started From*
$9.95 96 pages
1-880166-03-8 1992

Canio's Editions
P.O. Box 1962
Sag Harbor, New York 11963
Canio Pavone
(516) 725-4926

Anthony Brandt
The People Along the Sand
$9.95 83 pages
0-9630164-1-5 May 1992

Dan Giancola
*Powder and Echo: Poems About
the American Revolutionary War
on Long Island*
$9.95 37 pages
0-9630164-0-7 August 1991

Capra Press
P.O. Box 2068
Santa Barbara, California 93105
Noel Young, Editor;
Cynthia Cornett, Assistant Editor
(805) 966-4590

Tess Gallagher
Portable Kisses: Love Poems
$8.95 80 pages
0-88496-342-X February 1992

Carnegie Mellon University Press
Baker Hall, Box 30
Pittsburgh, Pennsylvania 15213
Irma Tani
(412) 268-6348
To order: Call (800) 666-2211

Window on the Black Sea:
Bulgarian Poetry in Translation
Edited by Richard Harteis
and William Meredith
$12.95 180 pages
0-88748-141-8 1992

Celo Valley Books
346 Seven Mile Ridge Road
Burnsville, North Carolina 28714
Diana Donovan
(704) 675-5918
Distributed by Baker & Taylor

H. J. Adams
The Eye of the Day and
Tooth of the Lion
$12.95, Cloth 48 pages
0-923687-18-1 May 1992

James Halon
Poetry
$12.95, Cloth 80 pages
0-923687-14-9 February 1992

Chelsea Green
P.O. Box 130, Route 113
Post Mills, Vermont 05058-0130
Chris Crochetiere,
Publicity Manager
(802) 333-9073

David Budbill
Judevine: The Complete
Poems, 1970-1990
$24.95, Cloth, 0-930031-47-4
$14.95, Paper, 0-930031-48-2
310 pages November 1991

Chicory Blue Press
795 East Street North
Goshen, Connecticut 06756
Sondra Zeidenstein, Publisher
(203) 491-2271
Distributed by Inland

Sondra Zeidenstein
Late Afternoon Woman
$4.95 40 pages
0-9619111-3-1 March 1992

Heart of the Flower: Poems
for the Sensuous Gardener
Edited by Sondra Zeidenstein
$13.95 102 pages
0-9619111-2-3 September 1991

Chiron Review Press
Rt. 2 Box 111
St. John, Kansas 67576
Michael Hathaway, Editor

Connie Edwards
The Girl That Time Passed By
40 pages
0-943795-17-6 1991

Marael Johnson
Mad Woman Bad Reputation
56 pages
0-943795-16-8 1991

Chronicle Books
275 5th Street
San Francisco, California 94103
(415) 777-7240
(415) 777-8887 FAX
Distributed by: Ingram;
Baker & Taylor

Francisco X. Alarcón
Snake Poems
162 pages
0-8118-0161-6 1992

City Lights Books
261 Columbus Avenue
San Francisco, California 94133
Lawrence Ferlinghetti,
Nancy J. Peters, Editors
(415) 362-1901
(415) 362-4921 FAX
Distributed by Subterranean

Gregory Corso
Gasoline
$6.95 104 pages
0-87286-008-4 June 1992

Charles Henri Ford
Out of the Labyrinth:
Selected Poems
$6.95 144 pages
0-87286-251-8 August 1991

Jack Kerouac
Pomes All Sizes
$8.95 192 pages
0-87286-269-0 June 1992

Vladimir Mayakovsky
Listen! Early Poems 1913-1918
Translated from Russian by
Maria Enzensberger
$5.95 64 pages
0-87286-255-0 August 1991

Clamshell Press
160 California Avenue
Santa Rosa, California 95405
D. L. Emblen
(707) 544-4532

D. L. Emblen
The Kenwood Suite
$10.00 30 pages April 1992

Don Greame Kelley
Don Greame Kelley
$31.50, Cloth 100 pages
1991

Clark City Press
P.O. Box 1358
109 West Callender Street
Livingston, Montana 59047
Debby Bull, Marketing Director
(406) 222-3371
To order: Call (800) 835-0814
Distributed by Consortium

Dan Gerber
*A Last Bridge Home: New
and Selected Poems*
$23.95, Cloth, 0-944439-38-1
$12.95, Paper, 0-944439-28-4
176 pages 1992

Greg Keeler
Epiphany at Goofy's Gas
$9.95 128 pages
0-944439-25-X 1991

**Cleveland State University
Poetry Center**
Department of English
Cleveland State University
Cleveland, Ohio 44115
Nuala Archer, Director
(216) 687-3986
Distributed by: Inland;
Spring Church

Red Hawk
*The Sioux Dog Dance: shunk
ah weh*
$8.00 60 pages
0-914946-90-0 December 1991

Robert Kendall
A Wandering City
$12.00, Cloth, 0-914946-86-2
$8.00, Paper, 0-914946-87-0
74 pages January 1992

P. H. Liotta
Rules of Engagement
$15.00, Cloth, 0-914946-88-9
$10.00, Paper 0-914946-89-7
137 pages November 1991

Eric Trethewey
Evening Knowledge
$12.00, Cloth, 0-914946-93-5
$8.00, Paper, 0-914946-85-4
91 pages October 1991

Clockwatch Review Press
Department of English
Illinois Wesleyan University
Bloomington, Illinois
61702-2900
James Plath, Publisher
(309) 556-3352

Martha M. Vertreace
Under a Cat's-Eye Moon
$28.00, Cloth, 0-914403-01-X
$5.95, Paper, 0-914403-00-1
80 pages September 1991

Coffee House Press
27 North 4th Street #400
Minneapolis, Minnesota 55401
Sandra Kalagian, Marketing Asst.
(612) 338-0125

Andrei Codrescu
Belligerence
$8.95 79 pages
0-918273-85-4 1991

Victor Hernández Cruz
Red Beans
$11.95 142 pages
0-918273-91-9 1991

George Evans
Sudden Dreams
$8.95 106 pages
0-918273-86-2 1991

Lawrence Fixel
Truth, War, and the Dream-Game
$10.95 167 pages
0-918273-88-9 1992

Leslie Simon
Collisions and Transformations
$9.95 124 pages
0-918273-93-5 1992

Robert Sward
Four Incarnations
$9.95 129 pages
0-918273-90-0 1991

Nice to See You: Homage to
Ted Berrigan
Edited by Anne Waldman
$24.95, Cloth, 0-918273-11-0
$14.95, Paper, 0-918273-13-7
252 pages 1991

Collier Books
(Division of Macmillan
Publishing Co)
866 Third Avenue
New York, New York 10022
Sharon Dynak
(212) 702-3425

The Best American Poetry 1991
Edited by Mark Strand
Series edited by David Lehman
$12.95 326 pages
0-02-069844-5 1991

Columbia University Press
562 West 113th Street
New York, New York 10025
Katherine Stebbins, Special
Sales
(212) 316-7131
(212) 316-9422 FAX

Lorrie Goldensohn
Elizabeth Bishop: The
Biography of a Poetry
$30.00, Cloth 306 pages
0-231-07662-2 Fall 1991

Saigyo
Poems of a Mountain Home
Translated from Japanese by
Burton Watson
$19.95, Cloth, 0-231-07492-1
$13.95, Paper, 0-231-07493-X
240 pages Fall 1991

Contact II Publications
Box 451 Bowling Green
New York, New York 10004
Josh Gosciak, Dan Bodah,
Maurice Kenny
(212) 674-0911
Distributed by SPD

Barbara A. Holland
*The Edwardian Poems & The
Queen of Swords*
$7.00 51 pages
0-936556-24-2

Paul Pines
Hotel Madden Poems
$7.00 51 pages
0-936556-25-0 1991

Copper Beech Press
Brown University
English Department, Box 1852
Providence, Rhode Island 02912
Randy Blasing, Editor
(401) 863-2393

Robert Cording
What Binds Us to This World
$9.95 71 pages
0-914278-57-6 December 1991

Jorge de Sena
Metamorphoses
Translated from Portuguese by
Francisco Cota Fagundes and
James Houlihan
$9.95 112 pages
0-914278-55-X October 1991

Copper Canyon Press
P.O. Box 271
Port Townsend,
Washington 98368
Mary Jane Knecht, Managing
Editor
(206) 385-4925

Stephen Berg
New and Selected Poems
$21.00, Cloth, 1-55659-044-X
$12.00, Paper, 1-55659-043-1
256 pages April 1992

Kay Boyle
Collected Poems of Kay Boyle
$10.00 176 pages
1-55659-039-3 October 1991

Hayden Carruth
*Collected Shorter Poems,
1946-1991*
$28.00, Cloth, 1-55659-048-2
$14.00, Paper, 1-55659-049-0
432 pages May 1992

Richard Jones
At Last We Enter Paradise
$10.00 80 pages
1-55659-042-3 November 1991

Pablo Neruda
The Book of Questions
Bilingual edition. Translated
by William O'Daly
$19.00, Cloth, 1-55659-040-7
$10.00, Paper, 1-55659-041-5
96 pages September 1991

Council Oak Books
1350 East 15th Street
Tulsa, Oklahoma 74120
Paulette Millichap, Publisher
(918) 587-6454

William Kistler
America February
$11.95 61 pages
0-933031-40-8 1991

Cross-Cultural Communications
239 Wynsum Avenue
Merrick, New York 11566-4725
Stanley H. Barkan,
Publisher/Editor
Bebe Barkan, Art Editor
(516) 868-5635
(516) 379-1901 FAX
Distributed by Baker & Taylor

Donald Everett Axinn
Dawn Patrol
Bilingual edition. Translated
into Italian by Nina and Nat
Scammacca
$20.00, Cloth, 0-89304-752-X
$10.00, Paper, 0-89304-753-8
96 pages June 1992

David Curzon
Midrashim
$15.00, Cloth, 0-89304-345-1
$5.00, Paper, 0-89304-346-X
48 pages February 1992

David Gershator
Elijah's Child
$15.00, Cloth, 0-89304-330-3
$5.00, Paper, 0-89304-331-1
48 pages May 1992

Maria Mazziotti Gillan
The Weather of Old Seasons
$15.00, Cloth, 0-89304-435-0
$5.00, Paper, 0-89304-436-9
48 pages May 1992

Steven Hartman
Pinched Nerves
$15.00, Cloth, 0-89304-202-1
$5.00, Paper, 0-89304-203-X
March 1992

Lance Henson
In A Dark Mist
Bilingual edition. Translated
into Cheyenne by the author
$15.00, Cloth, 0-89304-851-8
$5.00, Paper, 0-89304-856-9
20 pages April 1992 (Reprint)

Menke Katz
This Little Land
Bilingual edition. Translated
from Yiddish by Aaron
Kramer and Rivke Katz
$15.00, Cloth, 0-89304-325-7
$5.00, Paper, 0-89304-326-5
48 pages May 1992

Gabriel Preil
To Be Recorded
Bilingual edition. Translated from
Hebrew by Estelle Gilson
$15.00, Cloth, 0-89304-306-0
$5.00, Paper, 0-89304-307-9
48 pages April 1992

Gregory Rabassa
A Cloudy Day in Gray Minor
$15.00, Cloth, 0-899304-870-4
$5.00, Paper, 0-89304-871-2
48 pages June 1992

Mindy Rinkewich
The White Beyond the Forest
Bilingual edition including
original work in Yiddish and
English
$15.00, Cloth, 0-89304-762-7
$5.00, Paper, 0-89304-763-5
48 pages May 1992

Nikki Stiller
Notes of a Jewish Nun
$15.00, Cloth, 0-89304-316-8
$5.00, Paper, 0-89304-317-6
48 pages June 1992

Adam Szyper
And Suddenly Spring
Bilingual edition including
original work in Polish and
English
$15.00, Cloth, 0-89304-859-3
$5.00, Paper, 0-89304-860-7
48 pages April 1992

Leo Vroman
Love, Greatly Enlarged
Bilingual edition. Translated
from Dutch by the author
$25.00, Cloth, 0-89304-125-4
$15.00, Paper, 0-89304-126-2
112 pages April 1992

American Women Poets/
Amerikali Kadin Sairler
Bilingual edition. Translated
into Turkish by Talât Sait
Halman
$25.00, Cloth, 0-89304-071-1
$10.00, Paper, 0-89304-072-X
80 pages April 1992

Living American Poets/
Yasayan Amerikali Sairler
Bilingual edition. Translated
into Turkish by Talât Sait
Halman
$25.00, Cloth, 0-89304-073-8
$10.00, Paper, 0-89304-074-6
96 pages April 1992

Crown Publishers, Inc.
201 East 50th Street
New York, New York 10022
David Groff, Senior Editor
(212) 751-2600
To order: Contact the Sales
Department at (212) 572-2305

Out of This World: An
Anthology of the St. Mark's
Poetry Project, 1966-1991
Edited by Anne Waldman
$22.00 690 pages
0-517-56681-8 1991

Cummington Press
1803 South 58th Street
Omaha, Nebraska 68106
Harry Duncan, President
(402) 554-2715, 551-2312
To order: Contact Nebraska
Book Arts Center, Fine Arts
Room 210A , University of
Nebraska at Omaha, Nebraska
68182 (402)554-2773

Barry Goldensohn
Dance Music
$20.00 12 pages May 1992

William Wilborn
Rooms
$20.00, Cloth 80 pages
December 1991

Curbstone Press
321 Jackson Street
Willimantic, Connecticut 06226
Judith Ayer Doyle;
Alexander Taylor
(203) 423-9190
Distributed by InBook

Martín Espada
Rebellion Is the Circle of a
Lover's Hands
Bilingual edition. Translated
into Spanish by Camilo
Pérez-Bustillo and the author
$9.95 120 pages
0-915306-95-6 Spring 1991

Jack Hirschman
Endless Threshold
$10.95 123 pages
1-880684-00-4 1992

Luis J. Rodríguez
The Concrete River
$9.95 128 pages
0-915306-42-5 June 1991

Alfonso Quijada Urías
They Come and Knock on the Door
Bilingual edition. Translated
by Darwin J. Flakoll
$13.95, Cloth 64 pages
0-915306-99-9 April 1991

Clemente Soto Vélez
The Blood That Keeps Singing/La sangre que sigue cantando
Bilingual edition. Translated
from Spanish by Martín Espada
and Camilo Pérez-Bustillo
$9.95 128 pages
0-915306-78-6 September 1991

Cypress House Press
155 Cypress Street
Fort Bragg, California 95437
Cynthia Frank, President
(707) 964-9520

Adams
Passion of Creation
$9.95 132 pages
1-879384-11-6 March 1992

Lois Weikel
Expressions of Love, Faith and Humor
$11.00 64 pages
1-879384-14-0 May 1992

D

The Domestic Press
323 East 8th Street
New York, New York 10009
Stephen Shapiro
(212) 673-5903
Distributed by Inland

Stephen Paul Miller
Art Is Boring for the Same Reason We Stayed in Vietnam
$9.00 113 pages
0-934450-50-1 January 1992

Dufour Editions, Inc.
P.O. Box 449
Chester Springs, Penn 19425
Jeanne Dufour, Publicist
(215) 458-5005

Tony Harrison
A Cold Coming
$6.95 16 pages
1-85224-186-1 Fall 1991

E Publications
P.O. Box 19033
Washington, D.C. 20036
Eunice Lockhart-Moss, Publisher
(202) 223-4060
Distributed by Baker & Taylor

Frederick C. Tillis
Images of Mind & Heart
$14.95, Cloth 95 pages
0-944637-03-5 1991

Eagle Publishing
P.O. Box 403
Red Bluff, California 96080
Deborah Peterson
(916) 520-1126

Mando Sevillano
The Loneliness of Old Men:
Anthropoems
$8.95 80 pages
1-879027-01-1 January 1992

Eastern Caribbean Institute
Box 1338, 40 EG La Grange
Frederiksted, Virgin Islands 00841
S.B Jones-Hendrickson
(809) 772-1011
(809) 778-9168 FAX

S.B. Jones-Hendrickson
A Virgin Islands Sojourn?
$9.95 58 pages
0-932831-02-8

The Ecco Press
100 West Broad Street
Hopewell, New Jersey 08525
Bill Crager, Marketing Manager
(609) 466-4748
(609) 466-4706 FAX
Distributed by W.W. Norton

Louise Glück
Ararat
$9.95 68 pages
0-88001-248-X May 1992

Andrew Marvell
The Essential Marvell
Edited by Donald Hall
$8.00 128 pages
0-88001-312-5 November 1991

Czeslaw Milosz
Provinces: Poems 1987-1991
Translated from Polish by
the author and Robert Hass
$19.95, Cloth 72 pages
0-88001-317-6 November 1991

Robert Pinsky
The Want Bone
$9.95 72 pages
0-88001-251-X September 1991

Stanley Plumly
Boy on the Step
$9.95 64 pages
0-88001-229-3 October 1991

William Shakespeare
The Essential Shakespeare
Edited by Ted Hughes
$18.95, Cloth 230 pages
0-88001-313-3 October 1991

The Eighth Mountain Press
624 SE 29th Avenue
Portland, Oregon 97214
Ruth Gundle, Publisher
(503) 233-3936
Distributed by Consortium

Lori Anderson
Cultivating Excess
$18.95, Cloth, 0-933377-19-3
$9.95, Paper, 0-933377-18-5
128 pages May 1992

Empyreal Press
P. O. Box 898, Planetarium
Station
New York, New York 10024

Yukihede Maeshima Hartman
New Poems
$11.95 61 pages
0-921852-01-0 1991

Evanston Publishing, Inc.
1571 Sherman, Annex C
Evanston, Illinois 60201
Joan Pikas, Marketing Director
(708) 492-1911
Distributed by: Baker & Taylor;
Booksource

Johari Mashasin Rashad
*Steppin' Over the Glass: Life
Journeys in Poetry and Prose*
$9.95 80 pages
1-879260-05-0 March 1992

Gertrude Rubin
The Passover Poems
$8.00 48 pages
1-879260-00-X Spring 1991

Elaine Warick
Like a Hind Let Loose
$9.95 80 pages
1-879260-06-9 April 1992

F

Faber and Faber
50 Cross Street
Winchester, Massachusetts 01890
Betsy Uhrig, Editor
Anna Lowi, Marketing Director
(617) 721-1427
*To order: Contact the address
above or call 1-800-666-2211*
Distributed by Cornell
University Press Services

Rachel Hadas
*Unending Dialogue: Voices
from an AIDS Poetry Workshop*
$17.95, Cloth 156 pages
0-571-12943-9 Fall 1991

Primo Levi
Collected Poems: New Edition
Translated by Ruth Feldman
and Brian Swann
$10.95 128 pages
0-571-16539-7 Spring 1992

Christopher Reid
In the Echoey Tunnel
$9.95 96 pages
0-571-16254-1 Spring 1992

Harry Smart
Pierrot
$9.95 64 pages
0-571-16279-7 Spring 1992

*I Have No Gun but I Can
Spit: An Anthology of
Satirical and Abusive Verse*
Edited by Kenneth Baker
$12.95 205 pages
0-571-16235-5 Fall 1991

*The Faber Book of Twentieth
Century Scottish Poetry*
Edited by Douglas Dunn
$24.95, Cloth 400 pages
0-571-15431-X Spring 1992

Farrar, Straus and Giroux
19 Union Square West
New York, New York 10003
*To order: Contact the Sales
Department at (800) 741-6900*

David Ferry
*Gilgamesh: A New
Rendering in English Verse*
$15.00, Cloth 99 pages
0-374-16227-1 1992

Thom Gunn
The Man with Night Sweats
$15.00, Cloth 88 pages
0-374-20175-7 1992

Seamus Heaney
*The Cure At Troy: A Version
of Sophocles' Philoctetes*
$20.00, Cloth 81 pages
0-374-13355-7 1991
Seeing Things
$19.00, Cloth 107 pages
0-374-25776-0 1991

Christopher Logue
*Kings: An Account of Books 1
and 2 of Homer's* Iliad
$16.95, Cloth 86 pages
0-374-18151-9 1991

Federico García Lorca
Collected Poems
Bilingual edition. Edited by
Christopher Maurer
$50.00, Cloth 894 pages
0-374-12624-0 1991

Paul Muldoon
Madoc: A Mystery
$19.95, Cloth 261 pages
0-374-19557-9 1991

Herberto Padilla
A Fountain, A House of Stone
Bilingual edition. Translated by
Alastair Reid and
Alexander Coleman
$19.95, Cloth 109 pages
0-374-15781-2 1992

C. K. Williams
A Dream of Mind
$16.00, Cloth 100 pages
0-374-28894-1 1992

Adam Zagajewski
Canvas
Translated by Renata
Gorczynski, Benjamin Ivry
and C.K. Williams
$25.00, Cloth 81 pages
0-374-11867-1 1991

**Farrar, Straus and Giroux/
Noonday**

Joseph Brodsky
To Urania
$9.00 174 pages
0-374-52333-9 1992

Chase Twichell
Perdido
$10.00 69 pages
0-374-52342-8 1991

Derek Walcott
Omeros
$12.00 325 pages
0-374-52350-9 1992

**The Feminist Press at The City
University of New York**
311 East 94th Street
New York, New York 10128
Florence Howe, Publisher
(212) 360-5790
Distributed by Consortium

Grace Paley
Long Walks and Intimate Talks
Art by Vera Williams
$29.95, Cloth, 1-55861-043-X
$12.95, Paper, 1-55861-044-8
80 pages September 1991

Figure Eight Press
126 Western Avenue, Box 333
Augusta, Maine 04330
Harry Solomon
(207) 338-2474
Distributed by Inland; Bookpeople

Harry Solomon
Cycloid: A Circle of Poems
$12.00 80 pages
0-9630376-5-X Spring 1992

The Figures
5 Castle Hill
Great Barrington, Mass 01230
Geoffrey Young
(413) 528-2552

Clark Coolidge
Odes of Roba
$12.00 158 pages
0-935724-46-X September 1991

Clark Coolidge
The Book of During
$15.00 238 pages
0-935724-43-5 December 1991

Lyn Hejinian
Oxota: A Short Russian Novel
$15.00 292 pages
0-935724-44-3 October 1991

*That Various Field
for James Schuyler*
Edited by William Corbett
and Geoffrey Young
$7.50 56 pages
0-935724-51-6 November 1991

Firebrand Books
141 The Commons
Ithaca, New York 14850
Nancy K. Bereano
(607) 272-0000
Distributed by InBook

Dorothy Allison
*the women who hate me:
Poetry 1980-1990*
$8.95 69 pages
0-932379-98-2 1991

Eloise Klein Healy
Artemis in Echo Park
$18.95, Cloth 0-932379-91-5,
library edition only
$8.95, Paper 0-932379-90-7
82 pages 1991

Fithian Press
P.O. Box 1525
Santa Barbara, California 93102
Susan Daniel, Sales Manager
(805) 962-1780

R. Gabriele S. Silten
High Tower Crumbling
$8.95 168 pages
0-931832-86-1 October 1991

Jack Swansen
Verse Vote
$7.50 64 pages
0-931832-82-9 September 1991

Floating Island Publications
P.O. Box 516
Point Reyes Station,
California 94956
Distributed by Bookpeople; SPD

Diane Di Prima
Seminary Poems
$6.00 48 pages
0-912449-34-9 1991

Michael Hannon
Ordinary Messengers
$10.00 96 pages
0-912449-33-0 1991

Cole Swensen
Park
$8.00 64 pages
0-912449-40-3 1991

Stephan Torre
The Raven Wakes Me Up
$8.00 48 pages
0-912449-39-X 1991

Flume Press
777 Sierra View Way
Chico, California 95926
Casey Huff, Publisher
(916) 342-1583

Luis Omar Salinas
Follower of Dusk
$6.50 28 pages
0-9613984-6-9 September 1991

G

GLB Publishers
P.O. Box 78212
San Francisco, California 94107
W. L. Warner, Owner
(415) 243-0229

Robert Peters
Good Night, Paul
$8.95 75 pages
1-879194-06-6 December 1991
Snapshots for a Serial Killer:
A Fiction and a Play
$10.95 130 pages
1-879194-07-4 March 1992

Galiens Press
Box 4026, 524 West 23rd Street
New York, New York 10011
Assoto Saint, Publisher

Here to Dare
Edited by Assoto Saint
$10.00
0-9621675-2-5 June 1992

The Road Before Us: 100
Gay Black Poets
Edited by Assoto Saint
$10.00 192 pages
0-9621675-1-7 1991

Generator Press
8139 Midland Road
Mentor, Ohio 44060
John Byrum, Editor/Publisher
(216) 951-3209

Dick Higgins
The Autobiography of the
Moon: A Commentary on the
Hsin-hsin-ming
Published in one volume with
Seng-ts'an's *Hsin-hsin-ming*
Translated from Chinese by
George Brecht
$5.00 39 pages
0-945112-13-0 December 1991

Hank Lazer
Inter(ir)ruptions
$4.00 22 pages
0-945112-14-9 January 1992

Susan Smith Nash
Pornography
$4.00 24 pages
0-945112-15-7 March 1992

Gibbs Smith, Publisher/
Peregrine Smith Books
P.O. Box 667
Layton, Utah 84041
Lindsey Ferrari, Publicity
Sandra Dupont, Sales
(801) 544-9800
(800) 544-5502 FAX

Martha Collins
The Arrangement of Space
$9.95 64 pages
0-87905-390-9 September 1991

David Huddle
The Nature of Yearning
$9.95 64 pages
0-87905-459-X May 1992

Goats + Compasses
51 MacDougal Street, Suite 200
New York, New York 10012

Leonard Schwartz
Gnostic Blessing
93 pages
0-96223-909-7 1992

David R. Godine Publisher, Inc.
300 Massachusetts Avenue
Boston, Massachusetts 02115
Sally MacGillivray
(617) 536-0761, ext. 20

New American Poets of the Nineties
Edited by Jack Myers and
Roger Weingarten
$35.00, Cloth, 0-87923-892-5
$16.95, Paper, 0-87923-907-7
464 pages October 1991

Graywolf Press
2402 University Avenue, # 203
St. Paul, Minnesota 55114
Janna Raclemacher,
Marketing Associate
(612) 641-0077
Distributed by Consortium

Tess Gallagher
Moon Crossing Bridge
$17.00, Cloth 128 pages
1-55597-156-3 February 1992

Dana Gioia
The Gods of Winter
$9.95 62 pages
1-55597-148-2 1991

Eamon Grennan
As If It Matters
$19.00, Cloth, 1-55597-154-7
$11.00, Paper, 1-55597-155-5
96 pages January 1992

Cecilia Vicuña
Unravelling Words and the Weaving Water
Translated by Eliot Weinberger
and Suzanne Jill Levine
$12.00 160 pages
1-55597-166-0 1992

Great Elm Press
1205 Co. Rte. 60
Rexville, New York 14877
Walt Franklin, Publisher
(607) 225-4592

Walt Franklin
Uplands Haunted By the Sea
$8.00 90 pages
0-945251-10-6 Spring 1992

Great Lakes Poetry Press
Box 56703
Harwood Heights, Illinois 60656
Chuck Kramer, Publisher
(312) 478-1761
Distributed by: Baker & Taylor;
New Leaf

Step into the Light—Poems from Recovery
Edited by Chuck Kramer
$5.99 64 pages
0-925037-16-8 April 1992

Green Meadow Press
105 Betty Road
East Meadow, New York 11554
G. M. Frey (516) 794-5631

H

Joyce Araby
*Read My Lips, No More
Madonna Poems*
$3.00 24 pages March 1992

Alan Catlin
Down & Out in Albany, NY
$3.00 16 pages April 1992

John Sweet
The King of America $3.00
7 pages February 1992

Griffon House Publications
The Bagehot Council
P.O. Box 81
Whitestone, New York 11357
Dorothy W. Conte; Dolores
Frank
(718) 767-8380
*To order: Contact The
Bagehot Council above*

Anne Paolucci
*Gorbachev in Concert (and
Other Poems)*
$19.95, Cloth, 0-918680-42-6
$9.95, Paper, 0-918680-47-6
64 pages 1991

Hanging Loose Press
231 Wyckoff street
Brooklyn, New York 11217
Robert Hershon, Editor
(212) 206-8465
(212) 675-5239 FAX

Sherman Alexie
The Business of Fancydancing
$18.00, Cloth, 0-914610-24-4
$10.00, Paper, 0-914610-00-7
104 pages 1992

Kimiko Hahn
Earshot
$18.00, Cloth, 0-914610-84-8
$10.00, Paper, 0-914610-83-X,
96 pages 1992

Maureen Owen
Imaginary Income
$16.00, Cloth, 0-914610-98-8
$9.00, Paper, 0-914610-97-X
48 pages 1992

Michael Stephens
Jigs and Reels
$18.00, Cloth 0-914610-86-4
$10.00, Paper, 0-914610-85-6
104 pages 1992

Tony Towle
Some Musical Episodes
$18.00, Cloth 0-914610-38-4
$10.00, Paper, 0-914610-25-2
104 Pages 1992

Larry Zirlin
Under the Tongue
$16.00, Cloth, 0-914610-82-1
$9.00, Paper, 0-914610-81-3
80 pages 1992

Harcourt Brace
111 Fifth Avenue
New York, New York 10003
Irene Reichbach, Publicist
Suzanne Snyder, Publicity
Assistant
(212) 614-3000
*To order: Contact customer
service at (800) 543-1918*

Octavio Paz
In Search of the Present
1990 Nobel Lecture
Bilingual edition. Translated
from Spanish by Anthony Stanton
$8.95 68 pages
0-15-644556-5 Fall 1991
*The Other Voice: Essays on
Modern Poetry*
Translated from Spanish by
Helen Lane
$16.95, Cloth 160 pages
0-15-170449-X Fall 1991

Richard Wilbur
More Opposites
$12.95, Cloth 34 pages
0-15-170072-9 Fall 1991

First Light: Mother & Son Poems
Edited by Jason Shinder
$9.95 153 pages
0-15-631136-4 April 1992

*Tangled Vines: A Collection of
Mother and Daughter Poems*
Edited by Lyn Lifshin
$9.95 164 pages
0-15-688166-7 April 1992

Harlem River Press
625 Broadway, 10th Floor
New York, New York 10012
Deborah Dyson, Associate
Publisher
(212) 982-3158
(212) 777-4924 FAX
Distributed by: Inland;
Publishers Group West

Eugene B. Redmond
The Eye in the Ceiling
$12.00 181 pages
0-86316-307-6 1991

Saundra Sharp
Soft Song
$18.95, Cloth, 0-86316-301-7
$8.95, Paper, 0-86316-306-8
62 pages Spring 1991

Saundra Sharp
Typing in the Dark
$19.95, Cloth, 0-86316-300-9
$9.95, Paper, 0-86316-305-X
77 pages Spring 1991

Quincy Troupe
Weather Reports
$22.00, Cloth, 0-86316-003-4
$12.00, Paper, 0-86316-108-1
177 pages Fall 1991

Gloria Wade-Gayles
Anointed to Fly
$25.00, Cloth, 086316-304-1
$12.00, Paper, 0-86316-309-2
179 pages Fall 1991

HarperCollins Publishers
10 East 53rd Street
New York, New York 10022
Steven Sorrentino, Publicity
Director; Tracy Silverman
(212) 207-7000
*To order: Contact Customer
Service at (800) 331-3761*

Robert Bly
What Have I Ever Lost By Dying
$16.00, Cloth 112 pages
0-06-016817-X June 1992

Edna St. Vincent Millay
Selected Poems
Edited by Colin Falck
$18.00, Cloth 160 pages
0-06-016733-5 November 1991

Susan Mitchell
Rapture
$22.00, Cloth 90 pages
0-06-055320-0 April 1992

Frederick Rebsamen
*Beowulf: A New Verse
Translation*
$19.00, Cloth 109 pages
0-06-438437-3 October 1991

Kenneth Silverman
*Edgar A. Poe: Mournful and
Never-ending Remembrance*
$27.50, Cloth 564 pages
0-60-016715-7 November 1991

*Changing Light: The Eternal
Cycle of Night & Day*
Edited by J. Ruth Gendler
$18.00, Cloth 131 pages
0-06-016697-5 December 1991

**HarperCollins/Children's
Division**
10 East 53rd Street
New York, New York 10022
Barbara Olsen
(212) 207-7491
To order: Call (800) 331-3761

Barbara Esbensen
*Who Shrank My Grandmother's
House? Poems of Discovery*
$15.00, Cloth 47 pages
0-06-021827-4 1992

Christina Rossetti
*Color: A Poem by Christina
Rossetti*
Pictures by Mary Teichman
$15.00, Cloth 20 pages
0-06-022626-9 1992

Alvin Schwartz
*And the Green Grass Grew
All Around: Folk Poetry
from Everyone*
Illustrations by Sue Truesdell
$15.00, Cloth 195 pages
0-06-022757-5 1992

Red Dragonfly on My Shoulder
Haiku translated by Sylvia
Cassedy and Kunihiro Suetake
Illustrated by Molly Bang
$15.00, Cloth 30 pages
0-06-022624-2 1992

HarperPerennial
*(Trade Paperback Division of
HarperCollins)*

Susan Mitchell
Rapture
$11.00 90 pages
0-06-096906-7 1992

Sylvia Plath
The Collected Poems
Edited by Ted Hughes
$15.00 351 pages
0-06-090900-5 April 1992

Sylvia Plath
*Letters Home: Correspondence
1950-1963*
Edited by Aurelia Schober Plath
$15.00 502 pages
0-06-097491-5 April 1992

Henry David Thoreau
*The Winged Life: The Poetic
Voice of Henry David Thoreau*
Edited and with
commentaries by Robert Bly
$11.00 151 pages
0-06-097453-2 March 1992

Helicon Nine Editions
P.O. Box 22412
Kansas City, Missouri 64113
Joanne Riordan
(913) 722-2999
(913) 722-2999 FAX
Distributed by: Baker & Taylor;
Book Source; Inland

Biff Russ
Black Method
$9.95 55 pages
0-9627460-1-0 Fall 1991

HerBooks
P.O. Box 7467
Santa Cruz, California 95061
(408) 425-7493

Lesléa Newman
Sweet Dark Places
$8.95 109 pages
0-939821-01-X October 1991

Highland Acres Publishing
4586 North 95th Street
Lafayette, Colorado 80026
Vicki Hamer
(303) 666-4135

Vicki Hamer
Whispering Winds
$5.95 49 pages 1992

Henry Holt and Company
115 West 18th Street
New York, New York 10011
Judith Sisko, Special Markets
(212) 886-9324
(212) 633-0748 FAX

Yevgeny Yevtushenko
The Collected Poems:
1952-1990
Edited by Albert C. Todd with the
author and James Ragan
$29.95, Cloth 662 pages
0-8050-0696-6 1991

Homeward Press
P.O. Box 2307
Berkeley, California 94702
Wakean MacLean
(510) 845-7111
Distributed by: Bookpeople;
Inland; SPD

John Curl
Columbus in the Bay of Pigs
$4.95 82 pages
0-938392-10-7 November 1991

Host Publications
2510 Harris Boulevard
Austin, Texas 78703
Joe Bratcher, President
Elzbieta Szoka, Vice President
(512) 482-8229
Distributed by Inland

Anna Frajlich
Between Dawn and the Wind:
Selected Poetry
Bilingual edition. Translated
from Polish by Regina
Grol-Prokopczyk
$9.95 99 pages
0-924047-04-6 September 1991

Gerald Nicosia
Lunatics, Lovers, Poets, Vets
& Bargirls
$9.95 65 pages
0-924047-05-4 September 1991

Hot Pepper Press
P.O. Box 39
Somerset, California 95684
Hatch Graham, Publisher
(916) 621-1833

Patricia D'Alessandro
Croce d'Oro
$4.00 32 pages
1-880575-10-8 December 1991

Taylor Graham
After the Quake
$4.00 28 pages
1-880575-06-X December 1991
Aperture
$4.00 28 pages
1-880575-05-1 December 1991
Chances
$4.00 28 pages
1-880575-01-9 December 1991
Keeping the Sun Wake
$4.00 28 pages
1-880575-08-6 December 1991
Looking for Lost
$8.50 94 pages
1-880575-04-3 December 1991
Perishables
$4.00 28 pages
1-880575-03-5 December 1991
The Old Dog Plays Bass
$4.00 30 pages
1-880575-09-4 December 1991
Roadkill Collection
$4.00 28 pages
1-880575-02-7 December 1991

Houghton Mifflin Company
222 Berkeley Street
Boston, MA 02116
Mab Gray
(617) 725-5000
(617) 351-1109 FAX
*To order: Contact the Sales
Department at (617) 725-5000 or
call (800) 225-3362*

Scott Donaldson
*Archibald MacLeish: An
American Life*
$35.00, Cloth 600 pages
0-395-49326-9 1992

Andrew Hudgins
The Never-Ending
$17.95, Cloth, 0-395-58569-4
$9.95, Paper, 0-395-58570-8
67 pages 1991

William Matthews
*Selected Poems and
Translations, 1969-1991*
$19.95, Cloth 200 pages
0-395-63121-1 June 1992

May Swenson
The Love Poems of May Swenson
$9.95 85 pages
0-395-59222-4 1991

Hyperion
114 Fifth Avenue
New York, New York 10011
Lisa Kitei (212) 633-4495
To order: Call (800) 759-0190

David Rosenberg
*A Poets Bible: Rediscovering the
Voices of the Original Text*
$22.95, Cloth 410 pages
1-56282-988-2 1991

I

Ikon Inc.
P.O. Box 1355 Stuyvesant
Station
New York, New York 10009

Paul Pines
Pines Songs
$3.00 28 pages 1991

Andrew Gettler
*Footsteps of a Ghost: Poems
from Viet Nam*
$4.00 37 pages 1991

Tom Obrzut
Dark Clouds
$3.00 18 pages 1992

John Richey
For the Past Lifetime
$3.00 20 pages
1-877968-06-4 1992

Hal Sirowitz
Bedroom Wall
$4.00 34 pages May 1992

Chris Stroffolino
*Incidents (at the Corner of
Desire & Disgust): Poems
1985-1988*
$3.00 36 pages 1991

Mark Weber
Dig and Be Dug
$3.00 32 pages 1991

Iniquity Press/Vendetta Books
P.O. Box 1698
New Brunswick, NJ 08901
Dave Roskos
(617) 628-2061
*To order: Contact Low-Tech
Press at 30-73 47th Street,
Long Island City, NY 11103*

J

Mark Olson
The Woodcutter
$7.00 22 pages
1-55780-117-7 Winter 1991-2

**Jewish Women's Resource
Center**
National Council of Jewish Women
New York Section
9 East 69th Street
New York, New York 10021
Henny Wenkart, Series Editor

K

Grace Herman
Set Against Darkness
$9.00 71 pages
1-879742-06-3 1992

Kelsey St. Press
P.O. Box 9235
Berkeley, California 94709
Patricia Dienstfrey, Editor
(510) 845-2260
(510) 548-9185 FAX
Distributed by SPD

Juniper Press 1310
Shorewood Drive
La Crosse, Wisconsin 54601
John Judson, Owner/Editor
(608) 788-0096

Myung Mi Kim
Under Flag
$9.00 46 pages
0-932716-27-X October 1991

Shelley Ehrlich
Beneath All Voices
$30.00, Cloth, 1-55780-114-2
$12.00, Paper, 1-55780-113-4
71 pages Fall 1991

Rena Rosenwasser
Isle
Art by Kate Delos
$12.95 56 pages
0-932716-28-8 May 1992

Judson Jerome and Bruce Cutler
*Juniper Book 55 - Two Long
Poems*
$6.00 51 pages Fall 1991

Kitchen Table: Women of Color Press
P.O. Box 908
Latham, New York 12110
Barbara Smith, Publisher
Lillian Waller, Office Manger
(518) 434-2057
Distributed by Bookpeople;
Inland

Mitsuye Yamada
Camp Notes and Other Poems
$8.95 56 pages
0-913175-23-4 1992

Alfred A. Knopf
201 East 50th Street
New York, New York 10022
Sales Dept (212) 751-2600

Daniel Halpern
Foreign Neon
$19.00, Cloth 85 pages
0-679-40636-0 October 1991

Mary Kinzie
Autumn Eros and Other Poems
$19.00, Cloth 106 pages
0-394-58992-0 September 1991

Philip Levine
New Selected Poems
$15.00 288 pages
0-679-74056-2 May 1992
What Work Is
$10.00 80 pages
0-679-74058-9 May 1992

Cynthia Macdonald
Living Wills: New and Selected Poems
$21.95, Cloth 148 pages
0-394-58503-8 February 1992

J.D. McClatchy
The Rest of the Way
$10.00 80 pages
0-679-74059-7 May 1992

James Merrill
The Changing Light at Sandover
$30.00, Cloth 576 pages
0-679-41083-X May 1992
Selected Poems 1946-1985
$25.00, Cloth 352 pages
0-679-41082-1 May 1992

Sharon Olds
The Father
$20.00, Cloth, 0-679-41127-5
$11.00, Paper, 0-679-74002-3
80 pages May 1992

Michael Ondaatje
The Cinnamon Peeler
$19.00, Cloth 196 pages
0-679-40260-8 June 1991

Eric Pankey
Apocrypha
$19.00, Cloth 80 pages
0-679-40617-4 October 1991

Marge Piercy
Mars and Her Children
$20.00, Cloth, 0-679-41004-X
$11.00, Paper, 0-679-73877-0
176 pages April 1992

Stan Rice
*Singing Yet: New and
Selected Poems*
$23.00, Cloth 224 pages
0-679-41145-3 June 1992

Mark Strand
The Continuous Life
$10.00 80 pages
0-679-73844-4 May 1992
*Reasons for Moving Darker
& The Sargentville Notebook*
$11.00 108 pages
0-679-73668-9 February 1992

Mona Van Duyn
Near Changes
$10.00 70 pages
0-679-72909-7 February 1992

L

**Latin American Literary
Review Press**
121 Edgewood Avenue
Pittsburgh, Pennsylvania 15218
Yvette E. Miller, Poetry Editor
(412) 371-9023
Distributed by: Baker & Taylor;
Inland

Oscar Hahn
Love Breaks
Bilingual edition. Translated
by James Hoggard
$10.50 64 pages
0-935480-49-8 March 1991

Lodge Lane Press
P.O. Box 992, Knickerbocker
Station
New York, New York 10002
Alethea Cheng, Owner
(718) 789-8502

Robert Matson
Three Poems
Artwork by Alethea Cheng
$10.00 64 pages April 1992

Lorien House
P.O. Box 1112
Black Mountain, NC 28711-1112
David Wilson
(704) 669-6211

Al Beck
Gnomes & Poems
$10.00 75 pages
0-934852-59-6 January 1992

Los Hombres Press
P.O. Box 632729
San Diego, California 92163-2729
Jim Kitchen, Co-Publisher
(619) 688-1023
Distributed by InBook

Carol Montgomery
Starting Something
$6.95 45 pages
1-879603-01-2 January 1992

Lotus Poetry Series
c/o Michigan State University
Press
1405 S. Harrison Road, Room 25
East Lansing, Michigan
48823-5202
(517) 355-9543
To order: (800) 678-2120

James A. Emanuel
*Whole Grain: Collected
Poems, 1958-1989*
$25.00, Cloth 396 pages
0-916418-79-0 1991

*Adam of Ifé: Black Women in
Praise of Black Men*
Edited by Naomi Long Madgett
$15.00 235 pages
0-916418-80-4 January 1992

Louisiana State University Press
P. O. Box 25053
Baton Rouge, Louisiana
70894-5053
Michael Pakston, Promotion
(504) 388-6666

Greg Delanty
Southward
$14.95, Cloth, 0-8071-1733-1
$7.95, Paper, 0-8071-1734-X
48 pages April 1992

Brendan Galvin
Saints in Their Ox-Hide Boat
$14.95, Cloth, 0-8071-1694-7
$7.95, Paper, 0-8071-1695-5
43 pages February 1992

Cathryn Hankla
Afterimages
$14.95, Cloth, 0-8071-1684-X
$7.95, Paper, 0-8071-1685-8
54 pages November 1991

Robert Hazel
*Clock of Clay: New and
Selected Poems*
$14.95, Cloth, 0-8071-1738-2
$7.95, Paper, 0-8071-1739-0
57 pages February 1992

Pinkie Gordon Lane
Girl at the Window
$14.95, Cloth, 0-8071-1713-7
$7.95, Paper, 0-8071-1714-5
54 pages November 1991

Carole Simmons Oles
The Deed
$14.95, Cloth, 0-8071-1701-3
$7.95, Paper, 0-8071-1702-1
58 pages November 1991

Henry Taylor
The Horse Show at Midnight and
An Afternoon of Pocket Billiards
$19.95, Cloth, 0-8071-1777-3
$9.95, Paper 0-8071-1763-3
137 pages April 1992

Susan Wood
Campo Santo
$14.95, Cloth, 0-8071-1676-9
$7.95, Paper, 0-8071-1677-7
63 pages November 1991

Lovenut Press
194 Garfield Place
Maplewood, New Jersey 07040
K. Smith
(201) 762-7737

Edith W. McClinton
Stepping Out of the Fire
$6.95 80 pages
1-878846-05-1 May 1992

Kenneth L. Smith
Like the Fierce Winds of a Storm
His Life Must Rhyme-on
$6.95 60 pages
1-878846-03-5 June 1992

Luna Bisonte Prods
137 Leland Avenue
Columbus, Ohio 43214
John M. Bennett
(614) 846-4126

John M. Bennett
Fenestration
$2.50 10 pages
0-935350-33-0 1991

John M. Bennett and Johnny
Brewton
Somation
$2.00 16 pages 1992

S. Gustav Hägglund
In the Velvet Darkness
Jake Berry
The Tongue Bearer's Daughter
(Two chapbooks bound together)
$3.00 24 pages
0-935350-29-2/0-935350-28-4
1991

Sheila E. Murphy
A Rich Timetable and Appendices
Stacey Sollfrey
*Feeling the Roof of a Mouth
that Hangs Open*
(Two chapbooks bound together)
$3.00 24 pages
0-935350-30-6/0-925250-31-4
1991

M

Ediciones Mairena
1656 Peñasco Hills
Rio Piedras, Puerto Rico 00926
*To order: Contact Carmen D.
Lucca at 3131 Grand Concourse,
Bronx, New York 10468
(718) 367-0780*

Julia de Burgos
*Roses in the Mirror/Rosas en
el Espejo*
Bilingual edition. Translated
by Carmen D. Lucca
$10.00 140 pages
0-9623968-1-8 June 1992

MARCH/Abrazo Press
P.O. Box 2890
Chicago, Illinois 60690-2890
Carlos Cumpián,
Editor/Co-Publisher
Cynthia Gallaher, Assistant Editor
(312) 539-9638

Carlos Cumpián
Coyote Sun
$6.50 64 pages
1-877636-08-8 September 1991

Raúl Niño
Breathing Light
$6.00 48 pages
1-877636-10-X October 1991

Trinidad Sánchez, Jr.
Why Am I So Brown?
$8.00 112 pages
1-877636-03-7 October 1991

Ed Two-Rivers
A Dozen Cold Ones
$7.00 39 pages
1-877636-15-0 February 1992

Marc Zimmerman
*U.S. Latino Literature: An Essay
and Annotated Bibliography*
$10.95 158 pages
1-877636-01-0 April 1992

March Street Press
3413 Wilshire
Greensboro, North Carolina 27408
Robert Bixby

Stephen Dunning
Good Words
$6.00 24 pages
0-9624453-3-9 Fall 1991

Michael J. Gill,
The Atheist at Prayer
$6.00 24 pages
0-9624453-4-7 Fall 1991

Joan Payne Kincaid
You Can Hear the Darkness
Stirring
$6.00 35 pages
1-882983-02-5 Fall 1992

Ray Miller
Man Kidnapped by UFO for
Third Time
$6.00 39 pages
0-9624453-6-3 Fall 1991

Don Schofield
Of Dust
$6.00 27 pages
0-9624453-7-1 Fall 1991

Justin Spring
Other Dancers
$6.00 28 pages
0-9624453-5-5 Fall 1991

Russell Thorburn
The Company of Widows
$6.00 33 pages
0-9624453-2-0 Fall 1991

Marsilio Publishers
853 Broadway, Suite 1509
New York, New York 10003
Juan García, Managing Editor
(212) 473-5300
(212) 473-7865 FAX
Distributed by Consortium

César Vallejo
Trilce
Translated by Clayton Eshleman
$28.00, Cloth, 0-941419-50-9
$14.00, Paper, 0-941419-51-7
220 pages August 1992

Mayapple Press
P.O. Box 5473
Saginaw, Michigan 48603-0473
Judith Kerman, Publisher
(517) 793-2801

Evelyn Wexler
The Geisha House
$5.50 18 pages
0-932412-05-X May 1992

Mellen Poetry Press/
The Edwin Mellen Press
P.O. Box 450, 415 Ridge St.
Lewiston, New York 14092
Patricia Schultz, Marketing
(716) 754-2794, -8566

Robert Carter
the damp woods greening
$9.95 47 pages
0-7734-9659-9 April 1992

W. R. Elton
Wittgenstein's Trousers
$9.95 68 pages
0-7734-0020-6 December 1991

Cheryl Fish
Wing Span
64 pages
0-7734-9667-X 1992

Thomas Gardner
The Mime, Speaking
$9.95 58 pages
0-7734-0044-3 April 1992

Mark Goldman
*My Father's Spats and Other
Poems*
$9.95 64 pages
0-7734-9777-3 September 1991

Rochelle Lynn Holt
Warm Storm
$9.95 58 pages
0-7734-9790-0 October 1991

Lisa Kahn
*KPHTH: fertile and full of
grace*
Translated by Edna Brown
and Peter Kahn
$9.95 60 pages
0-7734-9437-5 January 1992

Norman Leer
I Dream My Father in a Song
$9.95 41 pages
0-7734-9453-7 February 1992

J. R. LeMaster
Journey to Beijing
$9.95 87 pages
0-7734-0030-3 March 1992

Ed Meek
Flying
$9.95 64 pages
0-7734-0040-0 April 1992

Gary Pacernick
Something Is Happening
$9.95 48 pages
0-7734-9439-1 December 1991

Patricia Claire Peters
When Last I Saw You
$24.95, Cloth, 0-7734-9619-X
$9.95, Paper
84 pages March 1992

Bertha Rogers
Sleeper You Wake
$24.95, Cloth, 0-7734-9669-6
$9.95, Paper
84 pages November 1991

Jan Zlotnik Schmidt
We Speak in Tongues
$9.95 65 pages
0-7734-000-1 November 1991

Lorne Shirinian
Earthquake
$9.95 73 pages
0-7734-9785-4 September 1991

R. A. Shoaf
Simple Rules
$9.95 55 pages
0-7734-0010-9 December 1991

Ted Thompson
Meetings with the Gods
$9.95 60 pages
0-7734-0014-1 February 1992

Augustine Towey, C.M.
The Things of Man:
Twenty-Four Poems (1990-1991)
$9.95 41 pages
0-7734-9474-X December 1991

Justin Vitiello
Vanzetti's Fish Cart
$9.95 78 pages
0-7734-0004-4 December 1991

Norman Weinstein
Suite: Orchid Ska Blues
$9.95 51 pages
0-7734-9441-3 December 1991

Merging Media
c/o Rose Shell Press
516 Gallows Hill Road
Cranford, New Jersey 07016
Rochelle L. Holt
(908) 276-9479

Rochelle Lynn Holt and Alex
Stach
Intersecting Orbits
$3.00 39 pages
0-934536-45-7 Spring 1992

Micah Publications
255 Humphrey Street
Marblehead, Massachusetts 01945
Roberta Kalechofsky
(617) 631-7601

Charlotte Mandel
The Marriages of Jacob—
A Poem-Novella
$10.00 110 pages
916288-32-3 October 1991

58

Midmarch Arts Press
300 Riverside Drive
New York, New York 10025
Cynthia Navaretta, Publisher
(212) 666-6990

Dante Alighieri
Images from Dante
Art by Lenore Malen
$14.00 30 pages
1-877675-08-3 1991

William Carlos Williams
Illuminations: Image for
Asphodel, That Greeny Flower
Art by Oriole Farb Feshbach
$20.00 86 pages
1-877675-09-1 1991

Milkweed Editions
430 First Avenue North #400
Minneapolis,
Minnesota 55401-1743
Teresa Bonner, Executive
Director (612) 332-3192
To order: Send to address
above c/o the Order Dept.

Lu Chi
The Art of Writing/Wen Fu
Translated from Chinese by
Sam Hamill
$6.95 57 pages
0-915943-62-X 1991

Patricia Goedicke
Paul Bunyan's Bearskin
$11.00 137 pages
0-915943-54-9 February 1992

Sam Hamill
Mandala
Art by Galen Garwood
$12.95 78 pages
0-915943-52-2 May 1991

Bill Holm
The Dead Get By With
Everything
$8.95 96 pages
0-915943-55-7 March 1991

Dennis Sampson
Forgiveness
$8.95 96 pages
0-915943-50-6 January 1991

Mixed Voices: Contemporary
Poems about Music
Edited by Emilie Buchwald
and Ruth Roston
$14.95, Cloth, 0-915943-82-4
$9.95, Paper, 0-915943-67-0
184 pages August 1991

William Morrow & Company
1350 Avenue of the Americas
New York, New York 10019
Skip Dye, Sales
To order: Call (800) 821-1513

Judith Hall
To Put the Mouth To
$19.00, Cloth, 0-688-11547-0
$8.00, Paper, 0-688-11546-2
80 pages 1992

James Seay
The Light as They Found It
$8.95 70 pages
0-688-10020-1 1991

Mother of Ashes Press
P.O. Box 66
Harrison, Idaho 83833-0066
Joe M. Singer, Poet-in-residence
(208) 689-3738

David Coy
Rural News
$8.95 54 pages
0-945009-04-6 1991

Moving Parts Press
70 Cathedral Drive
Santa Cruz, California 95060
Felicia Rice, Editor/Publisher
(408) 427-2271
(408) 458-2810 FAX

Francisco X. Alarcón
De Amor Oscuro/Of Dark Love
Bilingual edition. Translated
from Spanish by Francisco
Aragon with the poet
Drawings by Ray Rice
$280.00, Cloth 0-939952-09-2
$10.95, Paper, 0-939952-08-4
56 pages February 1992

Elba Rosario Sánchez
Tallos de luna/Moon Shoots
Bilingual edition. Poems in
Spanish and English by the author
Dra wings by Robert Chiarito
$300.00, Cloth
$10.95, Paper, 0-939952-12-2
44 pages June 1992

Maude Meehan
Before the Snow
103 pages
0-939952-10-6 November 1991

mulberry press
105 Betty Road
East Meadow, New York 11554
G. M. Frey
(516) 794-5631

Gina Bergamino
dream poems
$2.00 10 pages October 1991
The Reality Mother Goose
$2.00 19 pages March 1992

Gina Bergamino and
Lyn Lifshin
White Horse Cafe
$2.00 24 pages August 1991

G. W. Fisher
First & Third
$2.00 August 1991

Ignatius Graffeo
I Am What I See
$2.00 8 pages 1992

Scott Holstad
Street Poems
$2.00 15 pages August 1991

Tom House
I Ain't Retarded But
$2.00 8 pages August 1991

Ruth Moon Kempher
Nonnets
$2.00 12 pages August 1991

Lyn Lifshin
Between My Lips
$3.00 28 pages August 1991
Some Voices
$3.00 8 pages December 1991

Mark Magiera
Save the Barking Dog
$2.00 8 pages 1991

Tony Moffeit
Ghost Moon Over Pueblo
$3.00 28 pages August 1991

Todd Moore and Gina
Bergamino
American Cannibal
$3.00 20 pages April 1992

N

**New Directions Publishing
Corporation**
80 Eighth Avenue
New York, New York 10011
James Laughlin,
President/Publisher
(212) 255-0230
*To order: Contact W. W. Norton,
Sales Dept., 500 Fifth Avenue,
New York, New York 10110
(212) 790-4297*

Bei Dao
Old Snow
Bilingual edition. Translated from
Chinese by Bonnie S. McDougall
and Chen Maiping
$16.95, Cloth, 0-8112-1182-7
$8.95, Paper, 0-8112-1183-5
81 pages November 1991

René Char
Selected Poems
Bilingual edition. Edited by Mary
Ann Caws and Tina Jolas
$19.95, Cloth, 0-8112-1191-6
$10.95, Paper, 0-8112-1192-4
142 pages April 1992

Allen Grossman
The Ether Dome and Other Poems
New and Selected 1979-1991
$19.95, Cloth, 0-8112-1184-3
$10.95, Paper, 0-8112-1177-0
180 pages October 1991

Bernadette Mayer
A Bernadette Mayer Reader
$11.95 148 pages
0-8112-1203-3 May 1992

Octavio Paz
Sunstone/Piedra de Sol
Bilingual edition. Translated from
Spanish by Eliot Weinberger
$18.95, Cloth, 0-8112-1197-5
$8.95, Paper, 0-8112-1195-9
59 pages October 1991

Kenneth Rexroth
An Autobiographical Novel
Edited by Linda Hamalian
$14.95 542 pages
0-8112-1179-7 October 1991

Kenneth Rexroth
Flower Wreath Hill: Later Poems
$9.95 176 pages
0-8112-1178-9 October 1991

Dylan Thomas
On the Air with Dylan
Thomas: The Broadcasts
Edited by Ralph Maud
$22.95, Cloth 320 pages
0-8112-1209-2 April 1992

William Carlos Williams
The Collected Poems of
William Carlos Williams:
Volume 1, 1909-1939
Edited by A. Walton Litz
and Christopher MacGowan
$19.95 579 pages
0-8112-1187-8 September 1991

The Collected Poems of
William Carlos Williams:
Volume II, 1939-1962
Edited by Christopher MacGowan
$19.95 553 pages
0-8112-1188-6 September 1991

The Infinite Moment: Poems
from Ancient Greek
Translated by Sam Hamill
$9.95 108 pages
0-8112-1199-1 April 1992

*New Directions in Prose and
Poetry 55*
Edited by J. Laughlin, Peter
Glasgold and Griselda
Ohannessian
$24.95, Cloth, 0-8112-1180-0
$11.95, Paper, 0-8112-1181-9
231 pages November 1991

**New Poets Series Inc./
Chestnut Hills Press**
541 Piccadilly Road
Baltimore, Maryland 21204
Clarinda Raymond, Editor/Director
(410) 828-0724

Tony Esolen
Peppers
$6.95 64 pages
0-932616-37-2 Spring 1992

Carole Glasser Langille
All That Glitters in Water
$6.95 64 pages
0-932616-29-1 Fall 1991

Gail Wronsky
*Again the Gemini Are in the
Orchard*
$6.95 64 pages
0-932616-35-6 Fall 1991

New Press Chapbooks
53-35 Hollis Court Boulevard
Flushing, New York 11365
Bob Abramson
(718) 229-6782

John A. Todras
One Tough Mother
$2.00 16 pages December 1991

New Rivers Press
420 North 5th Street, # 910
Minneapolis, Minnesota 55401
C. W. Truesdale, Editor
Katherine Maehr, Managing
Editor
(612) 339-7114
Distributed by Talman

B. J. Buhrow
House Fire
$6.50 80 pages
0-89823-129-9 February 1992

Richard Lewis
*When Thought is Young:
Reflections on Teaching and
the Poetry of the Child*
$7.95 80 pages
0-89823-137-X June 1992

Maureen Seaton
The Sea Among the Cupboards
$7.00 72 pages
0-89823-134-5 February 1992

Mark Vinz
Late Night Calls
$8.95 160 pages
0-89823-138-8 June 1992

Patricia Zontelli
Edith Jacobson Begins to Fly
$6.50 80 pages
0-89823-133-7 February 1992

The Boundaries of Twilight:
Czecho-Slovak Writing from
the New World
Edited by C. J. Hribal
$14.95 354 pages
0-89823-121-3 1991

Nightshade Press
Box 76, Troy, Maine 04987
Carolyn Page
(207) 948-3427

Karen Blomain
Borrowed Light
$10.00 64 pages
1-879205-32-7 April 1992

Melody Davis
The Center of Distance
$7.95 72 pages
1-879205-30-0 May 1992

Carl Little
"3000 Dreams Explained"
$7.95 48 pages
1-879205-27-0 December 1991

Ronald Pies, M.D.
Riding Down Dark
$6.00 32 pages
1-879205-31-9 April 1992

Madeline Tiger
My Father's Harmonica
$8.95 48 pages
1-879205-09-2 September 1991

North Carolina Wesleyan
College Press
3400 North Wesleyan Boulevard
Rock Mount,
North Carolina 27804
Leverett T. Smith, Jr.
(919) 985-5193
Distributed by: Inland; SPD

Jeffery Beam
The Fountain
$8.50 72 pages
0-933598-32-7 Spring 1992

Roland Flint
Pigeon
$8.50 64 pages
0-933598-30-0 Fall 1991

Michael McFee
To See
Photographs by Elizabeth
Matheson
$24.95, Cloth 72 pages
0-933598-34-3 Fall 1991

Northeastern University Press
360 Huntington Avenue, 272HN
Boston, Massachusetts 02115
Jill Bahcall, Marketing Manager
(617) 373-5480
(617) 373-5483 FAX
To order: Contact Northeastern
University Press; c/o CUP
Services, Box 6525, Ithaca, New
York 14851

George Mills
The House Sails Out of Sight
of Home
$9.95 69 pages
1-55553-113-X November 1991

Northern Lights
493 College Avenue
Orono, Maine 04473
Michael Fournier,
Managing Editor
(207) 866-3561

Nancy Cardozo
Using the Natural Light
$7.95 80 pages
0-9621570-3-1 August 1991

Michael Fournier
Einstein
$4.95 32 pages
0-9621570-4 June 1991

Louis Ginsberg
Collected Poems
Edited by Michael Fournier
$37.95, Cloth 440 pages
1-880811-04-9 May 1992

Austin Hummell
Audible Ransom
$4.95 32 pages
0-9621570-8-2 December 1991

Kathleen Lignell
Red Horses
$7.95 64 pages
0-9521570-5-2 July 1991

Vernon Newton
Homage to a Cat
$9.95 64 pages
0-9621570-5-8 September 1991

Karl Shapiro
The Old Horsefly
$12.95, Cloth 64 pages
1-880811-05-7 May 1992

Deborah Stiles
Riding Limestone
$4.95 30 pages
1-880811-01-4 December 1991

Carroll F. Terrell
Ideas in Reaction: Byways to
the Pound Arcana
$12.95 236 pages
0-9621570-9-1 June 1991

W. W. Norton & Company
500 Fifth Avenue
New York, New York 10110
Jill Bialosky (212) 790-4297
*To order: Contact the Sales
Department.*

Agha Shahid Ali
A Nostalgist's Map of America
$17.95, Cloth 112 pages
0-393-03021-0 October 1991

A. R. Ammons
*The Really Short Poems of
A. R. Ammons*
$8.95 176 pages
0-393-30850-2 May 1992

Eavan Boland
Outside History
$9.95 152 pages
0-393-30822-7 1991

Carol Conroy
The Beauty Wars
$17.95, Cloth, 0-393-02920-4
$9.95, Paper, 0-393-30851-0
124 pages 1991

Norman Dubie
Radio Sky
$8.95 55 pages
0-393-30852-9 May 1992

Stephen Dunn
*Landscape at the End of the
Century*
$17.95, Cloth, 0-393-02972-7
$9.95, Paper, 0-393-30853-7
94 pages 1991

Greg Glazner
From the Iron Chair
$18.95, Cloth 112 pages
0-393-03098-9 May 1991

Mary Stewart Hammond
Out of Canaan
$17.95, Cloth 112 pages
0-393-03050-4 December 1991

Maxine Kumin
Looking for Luck
$17.95, Cloth 64 pages
0-393-03085-7 February 1992

Linda Pastan
Heroes in Disguise
$17.95, Cloth 96 pages
0-393-03006-7 September 1991

Susan Prospere
Sub Rosa
$18.95, Cloth 88 pages
0-393-03095-4 April 1992

Adrienne Rich
An Atlas of the Difficult World
$7.95 64 pages
0-393-30831-6 1991

Alberto Ríos
Teodoro Luna's Two Kisses
$9.95 96 pages
0-393-30809-X March 1991

Charlie Smith
*Indistinguishable from the
Darkness*
$17.95, Cloth 92 pages
0-393-02771-6 1991

Gerald Stern
Bread Without Sugar
$18.95, Cloth 117 pages
0-393-03094-6 April 1992

**W. W. Norton & Company/
Liveright Imprint**

E. E. Cummings
Complete Poems 1904-1962
Edited by George J. Firmage
$50.00, Cloth
0-87140-145-2 November 1991

O

Oberlin College Press
Rice Hall, Oberlin College,
Oberlin, Ohio 44074
(216) 775-8407

Marin Sorescu
*Hands Behind My Back:
Selected Poems*
Translated by Stuart Friebert,
Gabriela Dragnea and
Adriana Varga
$22.95, Cloth, 0-932440-58-4
$12.95, Paper, 0-932440-57-6
170 pages 1991

Orchises Press
P.O. Box 20602
Alexandria, Virginia 22320-1602
Roger Lathbury
(703) 683-1243

Gilbert Allen
Second Chances
$10.00 75 pages
0-914061-20-8 1991

Bruce Bennett
Taking Off
$10.00 84 pages
0-914061-26-7 1992

Michael Bugeja
Platonic Love
$10.00 80 pages
0-914061-21-6 1991

Mark Craver
*Seven Crowns for the White
Lady of the Other World and
Blood Poems*
$10.00 80 pages
0-914061-25-9 1992

Richard Foerster
Sudden Harbor
$11.95 96 pages
0-914061-28-3 1992

Richard Moore
No More Bottom
$10.00 75 pages
0-914061-22-4 1991

C. K. Williams
Helen
$50.00, Cloth 32 pages
0-914061-27-5 1991

Oxford University Press
200 Madison Avenue
New York, New York 10016
Ellen Chodosh, Trade
Paperbacks Director
(212) 679-7300
To order: Call (800) 451-7556

Basil Bunting
Uncollected Poems
$11.95 80 pages
0-19-282870-3 1991

Daniela Crasnaru
Letters from Darkness
Translated by Fleur Adcock
$10.95 64 pages
0-19-282883-5 1991

Gwen Harwood
Collected Poems
$14.95 232 pages
0-19-282882-7 1991

Sean O'Brien
HMS Glasshouse
$10.95 56 pages
0-19-282835-5 1991

Peter Porter
The Chair of Babel
$11.95 80 pages
0-19-282920-3 1992

P

Palmetto Press, Inc.
88 Glendale Drive
Miami Springs, Florida 33166
*To order: Contact Upstart Press,
19 West 73rd Street, Suite 4-A,
New York, New York 10023
(800) 358-POEM*

Jan McLaughlin and Bruce Weber
These Poems Are Not Pretty
$7.95 124 pages
0-9615619-9-8 April 1992

Papier-Mache Press
135 Aviation Way, #14
Watsonville, California 95076
Sandra Martz, Publisher/Editor
(408) 763-1420
Distributed by: Baker & Taylor;
Bookpeople; Inland; Pacific
Pipeline

Sue Saniel Elkind
Bare As The Trees
$12.00, Cloth, 0-918949-18-1
$8.00, Paper, 0-918949-21-1
116 pages April 1992

Parallax Press
P.O. Box 7355
Berkeley, California 94707
(510) 525-0101
Distributed by SCB Distributors

Judith Minty
Yellow Dog Journal
$8.00 63 pages
0-938077-85-6 Fall 1991

Miriam Sagan
True Body
$8.00 64 pages
0-938077-46-5 Fall 1991

Parsons Field Press
33 East 70th Street Apt 9C
New York, New York 10021
Robert M. Pennoyer

Victoria Parsons Pennoyer
Town House Gardens
77 pages 91-90494 1991

PASS Press
250 West 24th Street
New York, New York 11217
Allen J. Sheinman
(212) 691-7729

Valery Oisteanu
Moons of Venus
$10.00 48 pages
0-9601870-1-7 1992

Pennywhistle Press
P.O. Box 734
Tesuque, New Mexico 87574
Victor di Suvero
(505) 982-2622

Edith A. Jenkins
The Width of a Vibrato
$5.00 32 pages
0-938631-10-1 April 1991

Penumbra Press
P.O. Box 5144
Rockford, Illinois 61125
Christian Nelson

Gina Bergamino
*When You Read This You'll
Know Who You Are*
$2.00 10 pages August 1991
Kumquat Meringue
$3.00 32 pages December 1991

Perivale Press
13830 Erwin Street
Van Nuys,
California 91401-2914
Lawrence P. Spingarn,
Publisher (818) 785-4671
Distributed by SPD

Sheila Hellman
Positions
$5.00 23 pages
0-912288-32-9 April 1992

Persea Books
60 Madison Avenue
New York, New York 10010
(212) 779-7668

Vicent Andrés Estellés
Nights that Make the Night
Translated from Catalan by
David H. Rosenthal
$9.95 80 pages
0-89255-172-0 1992

Thylias Moss
*Rainbow Remnants in Rock
Bottom Ghetto Sky*
$9.95 71 pages
0-89255-157-7 1991

James Richardson
As If
$9.95 78 pages
0-89255-171-2 1992

*Poets for Life: Seventy-Six
Poets Respond to AIDS*
Edited by Michael Klein
$11.95 248 pages
0-89255-170-4 1992

Philomel Books
200 Madison Avenue
New York, New York 10016
Laura Walsh, Editorial Assistant
(212) 951-8712
Distributed by Putnam

Joseph Bruchac and
Jonathan London
*Thirteen Moons on a Turtle's
Back: A Native American
Year of Moons*
Illustrated by Thomas Locker
$15.95, Cloth 32 pages
0-399-22141-7 March 1992

Nancy White Carlstrom
Goodbye Geese
Illustrated by Ed Young
$14.95, Cloth
0-399-21832-7 October 1991

Pig Iron Press
P.O. Box 237
Youngstown, Ohio 44501
Jim Villani, Editor/Publisher
(216) 783-1269

The Epistolary Form & the
Letter as Artifact
Edited by Jim Villani and
Naton Leslie
$9.95 128 pages
0-917530-27-6 August 1991

Pinched Nerves Press
1610 Avenue P #6B
Brooklyn, New York 11229
Steve Hartman,
Editor/Publisher
(718) 998-0854

Stanley Nelson
Ode for Giorgio De Chirico
$1.00 2 pages
March 1992

Plain View Press
P.O. Box 33311
Austin, Texas 78764
Susan Bright, Publisher
(512) 441-2452

Susan Bright
Tirades and Evidence of Grace
$12.95 158 pages
0-911051-58-9 1992

Mary Esther Frederick
Elaine O'Brien, Cynthia J.
Harper, Pamela Rutherford
and Hazel Ward
How Many Moons
$11.95 111 pages
0-911051-61-9 1992

Plowman Press
Box 414, Whitby
Ontario, Canada L1N 5S4
To order: Contact G. M.
Frey at 105 Betty Road, East
Meadow, New York 11554

Gina Bergamino
Black & Blue Holiday
$4.00 32 pages
1-55072-023-6

Pocahontas Press, Inc.
P.O. Drawer F
Blacksburg, Virginia 24063-1020
Mary C. Holliman,
President/Publisher
(703) 951-0467

Elaine V. Emans
Love Letter to the Blue Planet
$5.95 84 pages
0-936015-29-2 February 1992

The Poet Tree/New Spirit/
I.O.T.A.
82-34 138 Street #6F
Kew Gardens, New York 11435
Ignatius Graffeo,
Editor/Director
(718) 847-1482

Marie Asner
Man of Miracles
$3.00 16 pages
March 1992

Gina Bergamino
In This Village We Join Hands
$3.00 20 pages
January 1992
The Emerald Sky
$3.00 20 pages
April 1992

Elaine Dallman
Movement
$3.00 20 pages
January 1992

Reginald Elliott Gaines
24-7-365
$5.00 28 pages
January 1992
Headrhyme Lines
$3.00 24 pages
May 1992

Ignatius Graffeo
Ghostwalk
$3.00 12 pages
March 1992
A Forest for the Trees
$3.00 24 pages
December 1991
Lampblack & Whiteout
$3.00 20 pages
February 1992
Ravens and Nightingales
$5.00 44 pages
October 1991
*Stamps—The Found Poems
of Elvis*
$3.00 16 pages May 1992

Rochelle Lynn Holt
Hymn of Existence
$3.00 12 pages
April 1992

Susan Hornik
Dedicated to the One I Drink
$3.00 16 pages
January 1992

Lyn Lifshin
Appletree Lane
$3.00 20 pages
April 1992

William J. Rice
*A Poem Immediately
Belongs to All*
$3.00 24 pages
February 1992

Adam Szyper
The Harvest
$3.00 20 pages
May 1992

Poetic Page
P.O. Box 71192
Madison Heights, Michigan
48071-0192
Denise Martinson, Editor/Publisher
(313) 548-0865

Phil Eisenberg
Above and Beyond
$6.00 40 pages
1-879533-05-7 September 1991

72

Daniel Gallik
A Blue That Speaks of Heaven
$6.00 40 pages
1-879533-06-5 September 1991

Patricia A. Lawrence
In the Wind's Eye
$6.00 40 pages
1-879533-07-3 September 1991

Denise Martinson
Forging a Foundation
$6.00 35-40 pages
1-879533-08-1 February 1992

Poetry Harbor
1028 East 6th Street
Duluth, Minnesota 55805
Patrick McKinnon,
Artistic Director
(218) 728-3728

Poets Who Haven't Moved to St. Paul
Edited by Patrick
McKinnon, Ellie Schoenfeld
and Andrea McKinnon
$7.95 73 pages
September 1991

Bern Porter International
22 Salmond
Belfast, Maine 04915
Bern Porter, Chairman of Board
(207) 338-6789
To order: Contact Tilbury House at 32 Water Street, Gardiner, Maine 04345

Janelle Viglini
The Magic Fillmore Fagin
$7.50, Cloth 32 pages
0-911156-45-2 April 1992

Poseidon Press
(Division of Simon & Schuster)
1230 Avenue of Americas
New York, New York 10020
Victoria Meyer,
Publicity Director
(212) 698-7000

To Woo & To Wed: Poets on Love & Marriage
Edited by Michael Blumenthal
$19.50, Cloth 266 pages
0-671-72347-2 1992

Potes & Poets
181 Edgemont Avenue
Elmwood, Connecticut 06110
Peter Ganick, Editor
(203) 233-2023

Martine Bellen
Places People Dare Not Enter
$8.00 69 pages
0-937013-40-4 1991

Paul Buck
no title
$8.00 62 pages
0-937013-38-2 1991

Rachel Blau DuPlessis
Drafts
$9.50 94 pages
0-937013-37-4 1991

Spencer Selby
House of Before
$9.00 105 pages
0-937013-36-6 1991

Diane Ward
Imaginary Movie
$9.50 90 pages
0-937013-39-0 1992

Precision Press
P.O. Box 1506
Norwalk, Connecticut 06852
Laurie Hiller, Owner
(203) 847-8160
*To order: Contact the address
above or The Open Book Shop at
Unquowa Road, Fairfield,
Connecticut 06430*

Laurie L. Hiller
Visions of Wonder
$4.95 52 pages
0-9632332-0-3 May 1992

Press of the Nightowl
320 Snapfinger Drive
Athens, Georgia 30605
Dwight Agner, Proprietor
(404) 353-7719

Mary Ann Coleman
Recognizing the Angel
$30.00, Cloth, 0-912960-20-5
$12.00, Paper, 0-912960-19-1
59 pages August 1991

Puckerbrush Press
76 Main Street
Orono, Maine 04473
Constance Hunting,
Publisher/Editor
(207) 866-4868; 581-3832

Sonya Hess
Constellations of the Inner Eye
$8.95 77 pages
0-913006-48-3 1991

Deborah Pease
The Feathered Wind
$8.95 80 pages
0-913006-49-1 1991

Purdue University Press
1532 South Campus Courts,
Bldg B
West Lafayette, Indiana
47907-1532
Donna Van Leer
(317) 494-2038

Richard Cecil
Alcatraz
$8.50 94 pages
1-55753-015-7 1992

Pushcart Press
P.O. Box 380
Wainscott, New York 11975
Bill Henderson, Editor
Distributed by W. W. Norton
& Company

The Pushcart Prize, XVI:
1991/1992 Best of the
Small Presses
Edited by Bill Henderson
$28.50, Cloth 573 pages
0-916366-71-5 1991

Pyncheon House
6 University Drive, Suite 105
Amherst, Massachusetts 01002
David R. Rhodes, President

F. D. Reeve
Concrete Music
$18.00, Cloth, 1-8811-1956-4
$11.00, Paper, 1-8811-1972-6
77 pages 1992

Quarry Press
P.O. Box 1061, Kingston
Ontario, Canada K7L4Y5
Bob Hilderley, Publisher
Melanie Dugan, Managing Editor
(613) 548-8429

Allan Brown
The Burden of Jonah ben Amittai
$11.95 64 pages
1-55082-022-2 September 1992

Nadine McInnis
The Litmus Body
$11.95 86 pages
1-55082-037-0 March 1992

Colin Morton
How to Be Born Again
$11.95 94 pages
1-55082-036-2 March 1992

R

Sandra Nicholls
The Untidy Bride
$11.95 68 pages
1-55082-021-4 September 1991

Rabeth Publishing Company
P.O. Box 171
Kirksville, Missouri 63501
Betty Quigley, Editor
(816) 665-8209

**The Quarterly Review of
Literature Poetry Series**
26 Haslet Avenue
Princeton, New Jersey 08540
Renee Weiss (609) 921-6976

Jane Finley Wilson
Poems for Life
$4.95 100 pages
0-9626735-4-4 February 1992

Bruce Bond,
The Anteroom of Paradise
B. H. Fairchild,
Local Knowledge
Judith Kroll,
Our Elephant & That Child
Geraldine C. Little,
W*omen: In the Mask and Beyond*
Jean Nordhaus,
My Life in Hiding
(Five book-length works
bound together)
$10.00
0033-5819 1991

Red Dust
P. O. Box 630
New York, New York 10028
Joanna Gunderson
(212) 348-4388

Joseph Donahue
Monitions of the Approach
$3.00 16 pages
0-87376-067-0 1991

Albert Mobilio
Bendable Siege
$3.00 16 pages
0-87376-068-09 1991

Red Herring Press
1209 W. Oregon
Urbana, Illinois 61801
Ruth S. Walker, Director
(217) 328-1530

Laura Hedin
Voices of Light and Grace
$5.00 47 pages
0-932884-19-9 Fall 1991

Dimitri Mihalas
Cantata for Six Lives and Continuo
$5.00 41 pages
0-932884-98-9 Spring 1992

Carmen M. Pursifull
*Elsewhere in a Parallel
Universe*
$10.00 121 pages
0-932884-99-7 Spring 1992

Ridgeway Press
P.O. Box 120
Roseville, Michigan 48066
M. L. Liebler, Founder/Publisher
(313) 577-7713

Michael Castro
(US)
$5.00 24 pages
1-56439-003-9 October 1991

Cheri Fein
Home Before Light
$5.00 28 pages
1-56439-002-0 September 1991

Linda Nemec Foster
*A Modern Fairy Tale:
The Baba Yaga Poems*
$5.00 20 pages
1-56439-014-4 January 1992

Joan Gartland
A Passionate Distance
$3.50 24 pages
1-56439-010-1 December 1991

Bob Hicok
Bearing Witness
$4.75 57 pages
1-56439-001-2 September 1991

M. L. Liebler
Deliver Me
$2.50 16 pages
1-56439-006-3 August 1991

Lawrence Pike
Pierced By Sound
$7.95 82 pages
0-925570-21-4 September 1991

John R. Reed
Stations of the Cross
$5.00 36 pages
1-56439-012-8 February 1992

Marc J. Sheehan
The Cursive World
$4.00 12 pages
1-56439-007-1 November 1991

*Labor Pains: Poetry from South
East Michigan Workers*
Edited by Leon Chamberlain
$8.95 80 pages
1-56439-009-8 November 1991

Rio Grande Press
P. O. Box 371371
El Paso, Texas 79937
Rosalie Avara, Editor/Publisher
(915) 592-4658

Make Mine Canine
Edited by Rosalie Avara
$4.95 26 pages 1991

Make Mine Feline
Edited by Rosalie Avara
$4.95 28 pages 1991

Say It with a Poem
Edited by Rosalie Avara
$4.95 47 pages 1991

Roof Books
(Division of the
Segue Foundation)
303 East 8th Street
New York, New York 10009
Ricardo Tarrega
(212) 674-0199

Charles Bernstein
Islets/Irritations
$9.95 101 pages
0-937804-47-9 1992

Jackson Mac Low
Twenties: 100 Poems
$8.95 103 pages
0-937804-42-8 1991

Melanie Neilson
Civil Noir
$8.95 94 pages
0-937804-45-2 1991

Ted Pearson
Planetary Gear
$8.95 74 pages
0-937804-43-6 1991

Rowan Mountain Press
P.O. Box 10111
Blacksburg, Virginia 24062
(703) 961-3315

Amy Tipton Gray
The Hillbilly Vampire
$5.00 40 pages
0-926487-04-3 Spring 1992

Clyde Kessler
*Preservations: A Collection
of Appalachian Poetry*
$5.00 30 pages
0-926487-00-0 Spring 1992

Runaway Spoon Press
P.O. Box 3621
Port Charlotte, Florida 33949
Or c/o Bob Grumman
1708 Hayworth Road
Port Charlotte, Florida 33592
Bob Grumman
(813) 629-8045

Michael Basinski
Red Rain Too
$3.00 12 pages
0-926935-64-X Fall 1991

Guy R. Beining
Vanishing Whores & the
Insomniac
$3.00 40 pages
0-926935-57-7 Fall 1991

Jake Berry
Equations
$3.00 42 p*ages*
0-926935-63-1 Fall 1991

Jonathan Brannen
Sunset Beach
$5.00 51 pages
0-926935-54-2 Fall 1991

Greg Evason
Nothing
$7.00 60 pages
0-926935-53-4 Fall 1991

Arnold Falleder
The God-Shed
$3.00 42 pages
0-926935-50-X Fall 1991

Bob Grumman
Of Manywhere-At-Once Vol 1:
ruminations from the site of a
poem's construction
$10.00 222 pages
0-926935-58-5 Fall 1991

Crag Hill
The Week
$7.00 55 pages
0-926935-59-3 Fall 1991

Karl Kempton
Charged Particles
$5.00 46 pages
0-926935-52-6 Fall 1991

David C. Kopaska-Merkel
underfoot
$3.00 48 pages
0-926935-60-7 Fall 1991

Richard Kostelanetz
Repartitions - IV
$3.00 20 pages
0-926935-67-4 Fall 1991

Jonathan Levant
Oedipus the Anti-Sociopath
(or autumn angst)
$5.00 30 pages
0-926935-62-3 Fall 1991

Damian Lopes
unclear family
$3.00 22 pages
0-926935-65-8 Fall 1991

John Martone
far human character
$3.00 17 pages
0-926935-56-9 1991

Michael Melcher
Parallel to the Shore
18 pages
0-926935-68-2 February 1992

Jack Moskovitz
Isis Slices
$3.00 34 pages
0-926935-66-6 1991

Thomas Wiloch
Night Rain
$3.00 54 pages
0-926935-55-0 1991

St. Lazaire Press
4 Patten Road
Rhinebeck, New York 12572
Bruce McClelland, Publisher
Distributed by SPD

Pierre Joris
Turbulence
$8.00 61 pages
1-880280-02-7 September 1991

Pat Smith
A Book of Ours
$8.00 64 pages
1-880280-01-9 September 1991

S

Sachem Press
P.O. Box 9
Old Chatham, New York 12136
Louis Hammer, Editor
(518) 794-8327
Distributed by: Baker & Taylor;
Inland

Rainer Maria Rilke
The Duino Elegies
Bilingual edition. Translated
from German by Louis Hammer
and Sharon Ann Jaeger
$9.95 91 pages
0-937584-15-0 December 1991

St. Martin's Press, Inc.
175 Fifth Avenue
New York, New York 10010
Karen Burke, Publicist
(212) 674-5151, ext. 540
*To order: Call Customer
Service at (800) 221-7945*

Ntozake Shange
A Daughter's Geography
$8.95 0-312-063-27-6
September 1991
nappy edges
$10.95 0-312-064-24-1
September 1991
*The Love Space Demands:
A Continuing Saga*
$15.95, Cloth, 0-312-05892-6
$9.95, Paper, 0-312-07627-4
64 pages May 1992

Saturday Press, Inc.
P.O. Box 884
Upper Montclair, New Jersey
07043
C. Mandel, Editor
(201) 256-5053

Dixie Partridge
Watermark
$7.00 80 pages
0-938158-11-2
November 1991

Doris Radin
There Are Talismans
$7.00 64 pages
0-938158-12-0
December 1991

Score Publications
125 B Bay View Drive
Mill Valley, California 94941
Crag Hill
(415) 388-0578

Bruce Andrews
Stand Point
$4.00 10 pages Fall 1991

Larry Eigner
A Count of Some Things
$3.00 4 pages Fall 1991

Spencer Selby
Stigma
$6.00 28 pages 1991

Sea Tree Press
Box 950
Briarcliff Manor, New York
10510
Pearl Bennette, President
(914) 941-8926

Adam Atkin
Alarms And Mirrors
$7.95 176 pages
0-9631360-3-8
December 1991

The Seal Press
3131 Western Avenue #410
Seattle, Washington 98721
Ingrid Emerick, Publicist
(206) 283-7844
Distributed by Publishers
Group West

Becky Birtha
The Forbidden Poems
$10.95 155 pages
1-878067-01-X March 1991

Barbara Kingsolver
Another America/Otra America
Bilingual edition. Translated
into Spanish by Rebeca Cartes
$14.95, Cloth, 1-878067-14-1
$10.95, Paper, 1-878067-15-X
103 pages March 1992

Segue Books
(Division of The Segue
Foundation)
303 East 8th Street
New York, New York 10009
Ricardo Tarrega
(212) 674-0199

Hank Lazer
Doublespace: Poems 1971-1989
$12.00 192 pages
0-937804-44-4 1992

Semiotext(e)
522 Philosophy Hall
Columbia University
New York, New York 10027
Prof. Sylvere Lotringer
To order: Contact Jim Fleming at
Semiotext(e), P.O. Box 110568,
Brooklyn, NY 11211

Eileen Myles
Not Me
$6.00 202 pages
0-936756-67-5 Fall 1991

Shambhala Publications
300 Massachusetts Avenue
Boston, Massachusetts 02115
Jennifer Pursley, Associate
Marketing Manager
(617) 424-0030

Matsuo Basho
Narrow Road to the Interior
Translated from Japanese by
Sam Hamill
$10.00 108 pages
0-87773-644-8 October 1991

Jalaluddin Rumi
Look! This Is Love: Poems of
Rumi
Translated from Persian by
Annemarie Schimmel
$10.00 112 pages
0-87773-541-7 October 1991

Beneath a Single Moon:
Buddhism in Contemporary
American Poetry
Edited by Kent Johnson and
Craig Paulenich
$20.00 358 pages
0-87773-535-2 November 1991

Only Companion: Japanese
Poems of Love and Longing
Bilingual edition. Translated
by Sam Hamill
$11.00 160 pages
0-87773-647-2 March 1992

Sheep Meadow Press
P.O. Box 1345
Riverdale-on-Hudson, NY 10471
(718) 548-5547

Allen Afterman
Kabbalah and Consciousness
$22.50, Cloth 129 pages
June 1992

Chana Bloch
The Past Keeps Changing
$10.95 78 pages
1-878818-15-5 May 1992

Aaron Rosen
Traces
$10.95 91 pages
1-878818-10-4 November 1991

César Vallejo
Trilce
Bilingual edition. Translated
by Rebecca Seiferle
$12.95 171 pages
1-878818-12-0 May 1992

B. R. Whiting
The Poems of B. R. Whiting
$10.95 96 pages
1-878818-08-2 May 1992

Singular Speech Press
Ten Hilltop Drive
Canton, Connecticut 06019
Don D. Wilson,
Editor/Publisher
(203) 693-6059

Petya Dubarova
Here I Am, In Perfect Leaf Today
Translated by Don D. Wilson
$8.00 64 pages
1-880286-07-6 April 1992

Susan M. English
Tapestry of Morning
$4.00 24 pages
1-880286-06-8 September 1991

Bina Goldfield
Blade Against the Skin
$5.00 32 pages
1-880286-04-1 September 1991

Stephen E. Smith
Most of What We Take Is Given
$8.00 64 pages
1-880286-05-X October 1991

The Spirit That Moves Us Press
P.O. Box 820
Jackson Heights, NY 11372-0820
Morty Sklar, Editor/Publisher
(718) 426-8788

Editor's Choice III: Fiction,
Poetry & Art from the US
Small Press (1984-1990)
Edited by Morty Sklar
$18.50, Cloth, 0-930370-40-6
$12.50, Paper, 0-930370-41-4
336 pages May 1992

Starlight Press
P.O. Box 3102
Long Island City, NY 11103

Ira Rosenstein
Starlight Poets 2: Sonnets
Edited by Ira Rosenstein
$5.00
0-9605438-5-6 May 1992

Naomi Shihab Nye
Mint
$5.00 27 pages
December 1991

Jeff Oaks
The Unknown Country
$5.00 32 pages
April 1992

State Street Press
P.O. Box 278
Brockport, New York 14420
Judith Kitchen, Editor
(716) 637-0023
Distributed by: SPD; Spring
Church

Israel Emiot
Siberia
Bilingual edition. Translated from
Yiddish by Leah Zazuyer and
Brina Menachovsky Rose
$10.00 68 pages
0-933581-05-X November 1991

Cecile Goding
The Women Who Drink at the Sea
$5.00 25 pages
April 1992

Dionisio D. Martínez
Dancing at the Chelsea
$5.00 28 pages
April 1992

Steam Press - Lad Publishing
5455 Meridian Mark, Suite 100
Atlanta, Georgia 30342
Myra Atkinson
(404) 257-1577

Stan Cohen
Beyond Hell
Art by Ed Ruscha
$750.00, Cloth, 0-9627440-4-2
$18.00, Paper, 0-9627440-5-0
72 pages 1992
Seeping Into/Out of the Well
Art by Gary Stephan
$750.00, Cloth, 0-9627440-2-6
$18.00, Paper, 0-9627440-3-4
1991
Two
Art by Glenn Goldberg
$1,100, Cloth, 0-9627440-0-X
$12.00, Paper, 0-9627440-1-8
48 pages 1991

Still Waters Press
112 West Duerer Street
Galloway, New Jersey 08201
Shirley Warren
(609) 652-1790

Kate Abbe
Joy Riding
$5.00 38 pages
1-877801-18-6 March 1992

Wick Edelhauser
Beneath the Wave
$6.00 32 pages
1-877801-19-4 May 1992

Jill McGrath
The Rune of Salt Air
$5.00 26 pages
1-877801-16-X November 1991

Shirley Warren
Somewhere Between
$5.00 36 pages
1-877801-17-8 October 1991

Stormline Press
P.O. Box 593
Urbana, Illinois 61801
(217) 328-2665
Distributed by Baker &
Taylor

Dan Guillory
The Alligator Inventions
$14.95, Cloth
0-935153-14-4 1991

Story Line Press
Three Oaks Farm
Brownsville, Oregon 97327-9718
Robert McDowell,
Editor/Publisher
(503) 466-5352
(503) 466-3200 FAX
Distributed by: Baker & Taylor;
Inland; Taylor Publishing
Company

Jeremy Driscoll
Some Other Morning
$10.95 116 pages
0-934257-66-3 1992

Gabriel Fitzmaurice
The Father's Part
$9.95 45 pages
0-934257-65-5 1992

James B. Hall
*Bereavements: Selected and
Collected Poems*
$14.95 112 pages
0-934257-63-9 1991

Mark Jarman
Iris
$16.95 126 pages
0-934257-88-4 1992

Sydney Lea
The Blainville Testament
$11.95 94 pages
0-934257-80-9 1992

David Mason
The Buried Houses
$10.95 95 pages
0-934257-84-1 1991

Lee McCarthy
Desire's Door
$10.95 83 pages
0-934257-85-X 1991

Ian McDonald
Essequibo
$10.95 63 pages
0-934257-90-6 1992

Brenda Marie Osbey
*Desperate Circumstance,
Dangerous Woman*
$9.95 105 pages
0-934257-57-4 1991

Vern Rutsala
Selected Poems
$16.95 281 pages
0-934257-61-2 1991

New Italian Poets
Bilingual edition. Edited by
Dana Gioia and Michael Palma
$16.95 385 pages
0-934257-42-6 1991

Subterranean Press
501 Francisco Street
San Francisco, California 94133
Peter Marti
(415) 474-9682

Peter Marti
Bitter Smoke, Holy Words
$4.00 36 pages
1-880060-00-0 December 1991

Marc Olmsted
Milky Desire
$4.00 36 pages
1-880060-01-9 December 1991

Suburban Wilderness Press
1619 Jefferson Street
Duluth, Minnesota 55812
Jennifer Willis-Long,
Associate Editor
(218) 728-3728

Patrick McKinnon
The Belize Poems
$3.95 27 pages
March 1992

Sun & Moon Press
6026 Wilshire Avenue
Los Angeles, California 90036
Douglas Messerli
(213) 857-1115

Bruce Andrews
*I Don't Have Any Paper So Shut
Up (Or, Social Romanticism)*
$13.95 312 pages
1-55713-077-9 June 1992

David Antin
Selected Poems: 1963-1973
$12.95 434 pages
1-55713-058-2 1991

Rae Armantrout
Necromance
$8.95 50 pages
1-55713-096-5 1991

Charles Bernstein
Rough Trades
$10.95 112 pages
1-55713-080-9 1991

Gloria Frym
By Ear
$9.95 80 pages
1-55713-083-3 December 1991

Jackson Mac Low
Pieces O' Six
$11.95 192 pages
1-55713-060-4 June 1992

Dennis Phillips
Arena
$10.95 174 pages
1-55713-127-9 May 1992

James Sherry
Our Nuclear Heritage
$10.95 264 pages
1-55713-126-0 December 1991

John Taggart
Loop
$10.95 238 pages
1-55713-012-4 December 1991

Sun-Scape Publications
65 High Ridge Road, Suite 103
Stamford, Connecticut 06905
Valerie Webster
(203) 838-3775

Kenneth G. Mills
Words of Adjustment
$13.95 113 pages
0-919842-09-7
June 1992

Sunflower University Press
1531 Yuma (Box 1009)
Manhattan, Kansas 66502
Carol A. Williams, Publisher
(913) 539-1888

George S. Bascom
Faint Echoes
$12.95 102 pages
0-89745-141-4 1991

Bert McDowell, Jr.
From Pilot to Poet
$14.95 144 pages
0-89745-137-6 1991

T

**Teachers & Writers
Collaborative**
5 Union Square West
New York, NY 10003-3306
Ron Padgett,
Publications Director
(212) 691-6590

Larry Fagin
*The List Poem: A Guide to
Teaching and Writing
Catalog Verse*
$11.95 201 pages
0-915924-37-4 Fall 1991

Tender Buttons
54 East Manning Street #3
Providence, RI 02906
LeeAnn Brown
(401) 454-4725
Distributed by SPD

Harryette Mullen
Trimmings
$7.00 72 pages
0-927920-02-6 1991

Rosmarie Waldrop
Lawn of Excluded Middle
$7.00 88 pages
0-927920-04-2 June 1992

Tesseract Publications
RR 1, Box 27
Fairview, South Dakota 57027
Janet Leih, Publisher
(605) 361-6942

Helen Eikamp
Fact 'n Fancy
$4.50 34 pages
877649-13-9 1991

Three Continents Press
P. O. Box 38009
Colorado Springs, Colorado
80957-8009
Dr. Donald E. Herdeck
(719) 579-0977

Jan Kemp
The Other Hemisphere
$18.00, Cloth, 0-89410-716-X
$10.00, Paper, 0-89410-717-8
68 pages September 1991

Muhammad Al-Maghut
The Fan of Swords
Translated from Arabic by May
Jayussi and Naomi Shihab Nye
$16.00, Cloth, 0-89410-685-6
$10.00, Paper, 0-89410-686-4
62 pages November 1991

Hilary Tham
Tigerbone Wine
$18.00, Cloth, 0-89410-727-5
$10.00, Paper, 0-89410-728-3
85 pages 1992

Tia Chucha Press
P.O. Box 476969
Chicago, Illinois 60647
Luis J. Rodriguez, Director
(312) 252-5321
Distributed by Inland

Jean Howard
Dancing in Your Mother's Skin
Photography by Alice Q. Hargrave
$12.95 67 pages
0-9624287-6-0 November 1991

Rohan B. Preston
Dreams in Soy Sauce
$6.95 64 pages
0-9624287-7-9 February 1992

Patricia Smith
Life According to Motown
$6.95 75 pages
0-9624287-2-8 Fall 1991

*Stray Bullets: A Celebration
of Chicago Saloon Poetry*
Edited by Ida Jablanovec, Susen
James and Jose Chavez
$9.95 108 pages
0-9624287-4-4 October 1991

Tilbury House, Publishers
132 Water Street
Gardiner, Maine 04345
Mark Melnicove, Editor-in-Chief
and Publisher
(207) 582-1899

Grace Paley
New and Collected Poems
$19.95, Cloth, 0-88448-098-4
$12.95, Paper, 0-88448-099-2
144 pages April 1992

Time Being Books
10411 Clayton Road,
Suite 201-203
St. Louis, Missouri 63131
Jerry Call
(314) 432-1771

Louis Daniel Brodsky
*Forever, for Now: Poems for
a Later Love*
$15.95, Cloth, 1-877770-28-0
$9.95, Paper, 1-877770-29-9
103 pages September 1991

Louis Daniel Brodsky
*Mistress Mississippi: Volume
3 of A Mississippi Trilogy*
$15.95, Cloth, 1-877770-36-1
$9.95, Paper, 1-877770-37-X
125 pages September 1992

William Heyen
Ribbons: The Gulf War - A Poem
$16.95, Cloth, 1-877770-44-2
$9.95, Paper, 1-877770-45-0
64 pages February 1992
Pterodactyl Rose: Poems of
Ecology
$15.95, Cloth, 1-877770-24-8
$9.95, Paper, 1-877770-25-6
68 pages September 1991

Timken Publishers, Inc.
225 Lafayette Street
New York, New York 10012
(212) 334-9550

John Yau
Big City Primer: Reading
New York at the End of the
Twentieth Century
Photographs by Bill Barrette
$25.00 131 pages
0-943221-13-7 1991

Top of the Mountain
Publishing
11701 South Belcher Road, # 123
Largo, Florida 34643-5117
Dr. Tag Powell
(813) 530-0110

John J. Ollivier
Fun With Irish Myths
$11.95 192 pages
1-56087-014-1 October 1991

TriQuarterly Books
Northwestern University
2020 Ridge Avenue
Evanston, Illinois 60208-4302
Gwenan Wilbur
(708) 491-7614
Distributed by Northwestern
University Press

Linda McCarriston
Eva-Mary
$10.95 80 pages
0-929968-26-3 1991

Muriel Rukeyser
Out of Silence: Selected Poems
$28.00, Cloth, 0-916384-11-X
$14.00, Paper, 0-916384-07-1
192 pages 1992

Trout Creek Press
5976 Billings Road
Parkdale, Oregon 97041-9610
Laurence F. Hawkins, Jr.,
Editor
(503) 352-4694

Bruce Holland Rogers
Tales and Declarations
$4.00 26 pages
0-916155-13-7 January 1992

Sam Silva
De La Palabra
$4.00 36 pages
0-916155-15-3 February 1992

Tsunami Editions
#6-1727 William St.
Vancouver, B.C.
Canada, V5L 2R5

Anne Tardos
Cat Licked the Garlic
$7.00 40 pages
0-921331-17-7 1992

Turnstone Press
607-100 Arthur Street
Winnipeg, Manitoba
Canada R3B1H3
Christine Paulos,
Marketing Director
(204) 947-1556
Distributed by Inland

Patrick Friesen
You Don't Get to Be a Saint
$9.95 96 pages
0-88801-163-6 Spring 1992

Roy Miki
Saving Face
$8.95 91 pages
0-88801-155-5 Fall 1991

Kathleen Wall
Without Benefit of Words
$8.95 56 pages
0-88801-161-X Fall 1991

Janice Williamson
Tell Tale Signs
$12.95 160 pages
0-88801-159-8 Fall 1991

U

United Artists Books
2616 Peter Stuyvesant Station
New York, New York 10009
Lewis Warsh
(718) 857-5974

Elio Schneeman
Along the Rails
$6.00 71 pages
0-935992-14 Fall 1991

Hannah Weiner
The Fast
$6.00 43 pages
0-935992-24-3 February 1992

University of Arkansas Press
201 Ozark Avenue,
Fayetteville, Arkansas 72701
Julianne Gronen, Assistant
Marketing Manager
(501) 575-3246
To order: Contact the
address above, Attention:
Order Department

David Baker
Sweet Home, Saturday Night
$16.95, Cloth, 1-55728-202-1
$9.95, Paper, 1-55728-203-X
96 pages July 1991

Gerald Barrax
Leaning Against the Sun
$16.95, Cloth, 1-55728-226-9
$8.95, Paper, 1-55728-227-7
61 pages April 1992

Dick Davis
A Kind of Love: Selected
and New Poems
$19.95, Cloth, 1-55728-216-1
$10.95, Paper, 1-55728-217-X
146 pages August 1991

Dan Masterson
World Without End
$16.95, Cloth, 1-55728-177-7
$8.95, Paper, 1-55728-178-5
71 pages 1991

Jo McDougall
Towns Facing Railroads
$16.95, Cloth, 1-55728-181-5
$8.95, Paper, 1-55728-199-8
64 pages 1991

Eric Nelson
The Interpretation of Waking Life
$16.95, Cloth, 1-55728-197-1
$9.95, Paper, 1-55728-198-X
81 pages 1991

Cesare Pascarella
The Discovery of America
Bilingual edition. Translated
from Romanesco by John DuVal
$17.95, Cloth, 1-55728-229-3
$9.95, Paper, 1-55728-320-7
120 pages December 1991

Frank Stanford
The Light the Dead See:
Selected Poems
Edited by Leon Stokesbury
$22.00, Cloth, 1-55728-192-0
$12.95, Paper, 1-55728-193-9
111 pages 1991

Julie Suk
The Angel of Obsession
$14.95, Cloth, 1-55728-246-3
$8.95, Paper, 1-55728-247-1
74 pages May 1992

University of Georgia Press
330 Research Drive
Athens, Georgia 30602-4901
David E. Des Jardines, Assistant
Marketing Manager
(706) 369-6130
To order: Contact the address
above, Attention: Sales Department

Casey Finch
Harming Others
$18.00, Cloth, 0-8203-1373-4
$8.95, Paper, 0-8203-1374-2
70 pages Fall 1991

Norman Finkelstein
Restless Messengers
$18.00, Cloth, 0-8203-1379-3
$8.95, Paper, 0-8203-1380-7
75 pages Fall 1991

Jonathan Holden
American Gothic
$20.00, Cloth, 0-8203-1408-0
$9.95, Paper, 0-8203-1409-9
65 pages Spring 1992
The Fate of American Poetry
$26.00, Cloth, 0-8203-1364-5
$12.50, Paper, 0-8203-1398-X
152 pages Fall 1991

University of Illinois Press
54 East Gregory Drive
Champaign, Illinois 61820
Susie Warren, Exhibits Manager
(217) 244-4703
To order: Contact the University of
Illinois Press at P.O. Box 4856,
Hampden Post Office, Baltimore,
MD 21211 or call (800) 545-4703

Jim Barnes
The Sawdust War
$12.95 136 pages
0-252-06239-6 1992

Lynn Emanuel
The Dig
$10.95 88 pages
0-252-06251-5 1992

Jean Garrigue
Selected Poems
$27.50, Cloth, 0-252-01859-1
$12.95, Paper, 0-252-06224-8
224 pages 1992

Barbara Helfgott Hyett
The Double Reckoning of
Christopher Columbus,
3 August -12 October 1492
$19.95,Cloth 136 pages
0-252-01866-4 1992

Edgar Lee Masters
Spoon River Anthology
Annotations by John E. Hallwas
$29.95, Cloth 464 pages
0-252-01561-4 1992

G. E. Murray
Walking the Blind Dog
$10.95 112 pages
0-252-06231-0 1992

University of Iowa Press
100 Kuhl House
Iowa City, Iowa 52242-1000
Peter Sims, Marketing Manager
(319) 335-2000
To order: Contact the Publications
Order Department, 100 Oakdale
Campus #M105 OH
Iowa City, Iowa 52242-5000

Philip Dacey
Night Shift at the Crucifix
Factory
$9.95 81 pages
0-87745-338-1 1991

Walter Pavlich
Running Near the End of the World
$9.95 87 pages
0-87745-358-6 1992

**University of
Massachusetts Press**
P.O. Box 429
Amherst, Massachusetts 01004
Ralph Kaplan, Marketing Manager
(413) 545-2217

Mark Halliday
Tasker Street
$20.00, Cloth, 0-87023-776-4
$9.95, Paper, 0-87023-777-2
276 pages May 1992

Joseph Langland
Selected Poems
$20.00, Cloth, 0-87023-747-0
$9.95, Paper, 0-87023-800-0
118 pages April 1992

University of Michigan Press
839 Greene Street
Ann Arbor, Michigan 48106
Diane L. Piel,
Exhibit Coordinator
(313) 763-0163 or 764-4430

David Lehman
The Line Forms Here
$32.50, Cloth, 0-472-09483-1
$12.95, Paper, 0-472-06483-5
240 pages May 1992

Jane Miller
Working Time: Essays on Poetry,
Culture, and Travel
$32.50, Cloth, 0-472-09480-7
$12.95, Paper, 0-472-06480-0
153 pages April 1992

University of Missouri Press
2910 LeMone Boulevard
Columbia, Missouri 65201
Karen Caplinger, Marketing
(314) 882-0180

Michael Blumenthal
The Wages of Goodness
$14.95, Cloth, 0-8262-0832-0
$8.95, Paper, 0-8262-0833-9
64 pages May 1992

Stephen Corey
All These Lands You Call
One Country
$14.95, Cloth, 0-8262-0837-1
$8.95, Paper, 0-8262-0838-X
64 pages May 1992

Judson Mitcham
Somewhere in Ecclesiastes
$14.95, Cloth, 0-8262-0802-9
$8.95, Paper, 0-8262-0803-7
64 pages December 1991

Stephanie Strickland
Give the Body Back
$14.95, Cloth, 0-8262-0809-6
$8.95, Paper, 0-8262-0810-X
64 pages November 1991

University of Nevada Press
MS 166
Reno, Nevada 89557-0076
Sandy Crooms, Marketing
Director
(702) 784-6573

Desert Wood: An Anthology
of Nevada Poets
Edited by Shaun Griffin
$27.95, Cloth, 0-87417-175-X
$14.95, Paper, 0-87417-181-4
256 pages November 1991

University of North Texas Press
P.O. Box 13856
Denton, Texas 76203-3856
Charlotte Wright, Editor
Barbara Edmanson,
Administrative Assistant
(817) 565-2142
To order: Contact University
Distribution; Drawer C; College
Station, Texas 77843-4354

Jerry Bradley
Simple Versions of Disaster
Texas Poets Series #3
$9.95 144 pages
0-929398-25-4 1991

Voices from Within
Edited by Nancy Jones
$9.95 120 pages
0-929398-37-8 1992

University of Notre Dame Press
P.O. Box L
Notre Dame, Indiana 46556
Kathy Moore, Marketing Manager
(219) 631-6346
To order: Contact the
University of Notre Dame
Press at P.O. Box 635, South
Bend, Indiana 46624

The Space Between: Poets
from Notre Dame, 1950-1990
Edited by James Walton
$19.95, Cloth 312 pages
0-268-01743-3 1991

University of Oklahoma Press
1005 Asp Place
Norman, Oklahoma 73019-0445
Jo Ann Reece,
Direct Mail Manager
(405) 325-5111
To order: Contact the
address above, Attention
Marketing

Michael Castro
Interpreting the Indian:
Twentieth-Century Poets and
the Native American
$12.95 221 pages
0-8061-2351-6 May 1991

Echoes of Egyptian Voices:
An Anthology of Ancient
Egyptian Poetry
Translated by John L. Foster
$19.95, Cloth 134 pages
0-8061-2411-3 April 1992

University of Pittsburgh Press
127 North Bellefield Avenue
Pittsburgh, Pennsylvania 15260
Sara Games, Advertising
and Publicity Coordinator
(412) 624-7945

Debra Allbery
Walking Distance
$19.95, Cloth, 0-8229-3687-9
$10.95, Paper, 0-8229-5458-3
64 pages September 1991

Maggie Anderson
A Space Filled with Moving
$19.95, Cloth, 0-8229-3704-2
$10.95, Paper, 0-8229-5467-2
63 pages April 1992

Sharon Doubiago
South America Mi Hija
$29.95, Cloth, 0-8229-3671-2
$15.95, Paper, 0-8229-5450-8
312 pages April 1992

Larry Levis
The Widening Spell of the Leaves
$19.95, Cloth, 0-8229-3675-5
$10.95, Paper, 0-8229-5454-0
77 pages September 1991

Louise McNeill
Hill Daughter: New and
Selected Poems
$29.95, Cloth, 0-8229-3685-2
$12.95, Paper, 0-8229-5456-7
168 pages October 1991

Peter Meinke
Liquid Paper: New and
Selected Poems
$29.95, Cloth, 0-8229-3681-X
$12.95, Paper, 0-8229-5455-9
120 pages October 1991

Kathleen Peirce
Mercy
$19.95, Cloth, 0-8229-3686-0
$10.95, Paper, 0-8229-5457-5
64 pages September 1991

University of Utah Press
101 University Services Building
Salt Lake City, Utah 84103
Susan L. Wakefield,
Marketing Manager
(801) 581-6771

Brewster Ghiselin
Flame
$7.95, 43 pages
0-87480-371-3 August 1991

Gwen Head
Frequencies: A Gamut of Poems
$17.95, Cloth, 0-87480-408-6
$10.95, Paper, 0-87480-395-0
140 pages May 1992

Eleanor Ross Taylor
Days Going/Days Coming Back
$7.95, 185 pages
0-87480-364-0 May 1991

University of Washington Press
P.O. Box 50096
Seattle, Washington 98145
Marcy Pirsch
(206) 543-4050

Chinese American Poetry:
An Anthology
Edited by L. Ling-chi Wang
and Henry Yiheng Zhao
$19.95 272 pages
0-295-97154-1 February 1992

Island: Poetry and History
of Chinese Immigrants on
Angel Island, 1910-40
Bilingual edition. Translated
by Him Mark Lai, Genny Lim
and Judy Yung
$14.95 174 pages
0-295-97109-6 July 1991

University of Wisconsin Press
114 North Murray Street
Madison, Wisconsin 53715-1199
(608) 262-8782
(608) 262-7560 FAX

Renée Ashley
Salt
$14.50, Cloth, 0-299-13140-8
$9.95, Paper, 0-299-134144-0
70 pages January 1992

Léopold Sédar Senghor
The Collected Poetry
Translated by Melvin Dixon
$40.00, Cloth 798 pages
0-8139-1275-X December 1991

University Press of Florida
15 North West 15th Street
Gainesville, Florida 32611
Cindy Tomas,
Exhibits/Marketing
(904) 392-1351

Urban Press
300 Commercial Street
Boston, Massachusetts 02109
Rufus Goodwin
(617) 367-2211

Jean Burden
Taking Light from Each Other
$17.95, Cloth, 0-8130-1113-2
$10.95, Paper, 0-8130-1114-0
96 pages February 1992

Rufus Goodwin
The Open Drawer
$12.50 106 pages
0-9628429-1-5 Spring 1992

William Hathaway
Churlsgrace
$16.95, Cloth, 0-8130-1125-6
$10.95, Paper, 0-8130-1126-4
106 pages February 1992

V

Judith Minty
Dancing the Fault
$16.95, Cloth, 0-8130-1079-9
$9.95, Paper, 0-8130-1080-2
86 pages July 1991

Viking Penguin
375 Hudson Street
New York, New York 10014
(212) 366-2000
To order: Call (800) 526-0275

University Press of Virginia
P.O. Box 3608, University Station
Charlottesville, Virginia 22903
(804) 924-3469

The Portable Beat Reader
Edited by Ann Charters
$25.00, Cloth 626 pages
0-670-83885-3 January 1992

Derek Mahon
Selected Poems
$20.00, Cloth 194 pages
0-670-83575-7 1991

W Space Press
138 Duane Street
New York, New York 10013
Coco Gordon
(212) 285-1609

Coco Gordon
Blip Blipped
$30.00 20 pages
0-943375-20-7 1991

Coco Gordon and others
*Artists Perform From Their
Ecological Source: Working
to Re-open Major Life Systems
of the Planet*
$25.00 37 pages 1991

Wake Forest University Press
P.O. Box 7333
Winston-Salem, NC 27109
Dillon Johnston, Director
Candide Jones, Manager
(919) 759-5448

Austin Clarke
Selected Poems
Edited by Hugh Maxton
$23.95, Cloth 288 pages
0-916390-50-0 September 1991

Michael Longley
Gorse Fires
$11.95, Cloth, 0-916390-49-7
$6.95, Paper, 0-916390-48-9
52 pages November 1991

Pierre Reverdy
Selected Poems
Bilingual edition. Translated from
French by John Ashbery, Mary
Ann Caws and Patricia Terry
$16.95, Cloth, 0-916390-47-0
$10.95, Paper, 0-916390-46-2
173 pages September 1991

Warthog Press
29 South Valley Road
West Orange, New Jersey 07052
Patricia Fillingham, Editor
(201) 731-9269

Patricia Fillingham
*Report to the Interim
Shareholders*
$10.00 104 pages
0-942292-11-1 1991

Washington Writers'
Publishing House
P.O. Box 15271
Washington, D.C. 20003
Jean Nordhaus
(202) 543-1905

Joseph Thackery
The Dark Above Mad River
$10.00 72 pages
0-931846-40-4 March 1992

Naomi Thiers
Only the Raw Hands Are Heaven
$10.00 72 pages
0-931846-41-2 March 1992

Wayne State University Press
5959 Woodward
Detroit, Michigan 48202
Ann Schwartz
(313) 577-6120

Margherita Guidacci
Landscape with Ruins: Selected
Poetry of Margherita Guidacci
Translated from Italian
by Ruth Feldman
$19.95 123 pages
0-8143-2352-9 June 1992

Ruth Whitman
Laughing Gas: Poems New
& Selected 1963-1990
$34.95, Cloth, 0-8143-2315-4
$19.95, Paper, 0-8143-2316-2
281 pages Fall 1991

We Press
P.O. Box 1503
Santa Cruz, California 95061
Christopher Funkhouser;
Stephen Cope
(408) 427-9711

Francisco X. Alarcón
Loma Prieta
$3.50 32 pages
0-9627192-1-8 1991

Elisabeth Belile
After With Hope
$2.00 31 pages
0-9627192-6-9 1992

Dave Cope
Coming Home
$3.50 8 pages
0-9627192-7-7 1992

Stephen Cope
to be alone is all there is
$1.00 8 pages
0-9627192-4-2 1991

Karl Daegling
uh oh
$1.00 13 pages
0-9627192-8-5 1992

Steven Taylor
Fragments
$3.00 12 pages
0-9627192-6-4 1992

Katie Yates
Reference
$3.00 14 pages
0-962192-3-4 1991

White Eagle Coffee Store Press
P.O. Box 383
Fox River Grove, Illinois 60021
Frank Smith
(708) 639-9200

Paul Andrew E. Smith
Scenes from the Postmodern
Butler
32 pages 1992

White Pine Press
10 Village Square
Fredonia, New York 14063
Dennis Maloney, Editor;
Lisa Fuller, Office Manager
(716) 672-5743
Distributed by InBook

Marjorie Agosín
Circles of Madness: Mothers
of the Plaza de Mayo
Bilingual edition. Translated by
Celeste Kostopulos-Cooperman
Photographs by Alicia D'Amico
and Alicia Sanguinetti
$13.00 128 pages
1-877727-17-2 1992

Roberto Juarroz
Vertical Poetry: Recent Poems
Translated from Spanish by
Mary Crow
$11.00 128 pages
1-877727-08-3 1992

John Montague
Born in Brooklyn: John
Montague's America
$10.00 120 pages
1-877727-13-X 1991

Tommy Olofsson
Elemental Poems
Translated from Swedish by
Jean Pearson
$9.00 72 pages
1-877727-09-1 1992

Wildflower Press
P.O. Box 4757
Albuquerque, New Mexico 87196
Jeanne Shannon,
Editor/Publisher
(505) 296-0691

Mary Rising Higgins, Karen
McKinnon, Alexis Rotella
and Jeanne Shannon
Queen Anne's Lace
$9.50 84 pages
September 1991

Willamette River Books
P.O. Box 605
Troutdale, Oregon 97060
Evelyn Sharenov, Senior Editor
(503) 667-5548

Martin Anderson
Swamp Fever
$4.50 31 pages
0-9627791-1-3 November 1991

Alana Sherman
Everything Is Gates
$9.95 50 pages
0-9627791-0-5 December 1991

The Winstead Press
202 Slice Drive
Stamford, Connecticut 06907
Frances McCall, Editor
(203) 322-4941

Jane F. Babson
Babson's Bestiary
$10.95 32 pages
0-940787-02-4 1991

The Write Technique
28 Vesey Street, Suite 2122
New York, New York 10007

*Perceptions, Volume II: A
Poetry Anthology*
Edited by Richard Bearse
131 pages 1991

Y

Yale University Press
92A Yale Station
New Haven, Connecticut 06520
Stan Forrester,
Exhibits Manager
(203) 432-0958

Nicholas Samaras
Hands of the Saddlemaker
$16.00, Cloth, 0-300-05457-2
$9.00, Paper, 0-300-05458-0
80 pages 1992

*Ovid's Heroines: A Verse
Translation of the Heroides*
Translated by Daryl Hine
$27.50, Cloth, 0-300-05093-3
$11.00, Paper, 0-300-05094-1
176 pages 1991

Yellow Moon Press
P.O. Box 381316
Cambridge, Massachusetts 02238
Robert Smyth, Publisher
Brenda Robb, Assistant Editor
(617) 776-2230
Distributed by: Bookpeople;
Inland

Ruth Stone
*Second-Hand Coat: Poems
New and Selected*
$10.95 131 pages
0-938756-33-8 Fall 1991
Who Is the Widow's Muse?
$10.95 59 pages
0-938756-32-X Fall 1991

Yellow Press
5819 N. Sacramento
Chicago, Illinois 60659
Distributed by SPD

Joel Lewis
House Rent Boogie
$5.95 64 pages
0-916328-21-X 1992

Z

Zoland Books
384 Huron Avenue
Cambridge, Massachusetts 02138
Roland F. Pease, Publisher
Christine Alaimo, Marketing
(617) 864-6252
Distributed by InBook

William Corbett
Don't Think: Look
$9.95 128 pages
0-944072-17-8 Fall 1991

Gary Fincke
*The Double Negatives of the
Living*
$9.95 96 pages
0-944072-18-6 April 1992

INDEX BY AUTHOR

E

Hamill, Sam. *Mandala.*
Milkweed Editions
——— (trans.).
Milkweed Editions
——— (trans.). *The
Infinite Moment:
Poems from Ancient
Greek.* New
Directions
——— (trans.). *Only
Companion: Japanese
Poems of Love and
Longing.* Shambhala
Publications

Hammer, Louis, et al.
(trans.). Sachem Press

Hammond, Mary
Stewart. *Out of
Canaan.* W.W Norton

Hankla, Cathryn.
Afterimages.
Louisiana State
University Press

Hannon, Michael.
Ordinary Messengers.
Floating Island
Publications

Harper, Cynthia J. *How
Many Moons.* Plain
View Press

Harrison, Tony. *A Cold
Coming.* Dufour
Editions

Harteis, Richard, et al.
(ed.). *Window on the
Black Sea: Bulgarian
Poetry in Translation.*
Carnegie Mellon
University Press

Hartman, Steven.
Pinched Nerves.
Cross-Cultural
Communications

Hartman, Yukihede
Maeshima. *New
Poems.* Empyreal Press

Harwood, Gwen.
Collected Poems.
Oxford University
Press

Hass, Robert (trans.).
Ecco Press

Hathaway, William.
Churlsgrace.
University Press of
Florida

Hawkes, John. *Island
Fire.* Burning Deck

Hazel, Robert. *Clock of
Clay: New and
Selected Poems.*
Louisiana State
University Press

Head, Gwen.
*Frequencies: A Gamut
of Poems.* University
of Utah Press

Healy, Eloise Klein.
Artemis in Echo Park.
Firebrand Books

Heaney, Seamus. *The
Cure At Troy: A
Version of Sophocles'
Philoctetes.* Farrar,
Straus and Giroux
———. *Seeing Things.*
Farrar, Straus and
Giroux

Heard, Georgia.
*Creatures of Earth,
Sea and Sky.* Boyds
Mills Press

Hedin, Laura. *Voices of
Light and Grace.* Red
Herring Press

Hejinian, Lyn. *Oxota: A
Short Russian Novel.*
The Figures

Hellman, Sheila.
Positions. Perivale
Press

Henderson, Bill (ed.).
*The Pushcart Prize,
XVI: 1991/1992 Best
of the Small Presses.*
Pushcart Press

Henson, Lance. *In a
Dark Mist.*
Cross-Cultural
Communications

Herman, Grace. *Set
Against Darkness.*
Jewish Women's
Resource Center

Hershey, Connie (ed.).
*Truth and Lies That
Press for Life: 60 Los
Angeles Poets.*
Artifact Press

Hess, Sonya.
*Constellations of the
Inner Eye.*
Puckerbrush Press

Kingsolver, Barbara. *Another America/Otra America*. The Seal Press

Kinzie, Mary. *Autumn Eros and Other Poems*. Alfred A. Knopf

Kistler, William. *America February*. Council Oak Books

Klein, Michael (ed.). *Poets for Life: Seventy-Six Poets Respond to AIDS*. Persea Books

Kopaska-Merkel, David C. *underfoot*. Runaway Spoon Press

Kostelanetz, Richard. *Repartitions - IV*. Runaway Spoon Press

Kostopulos-Cooperman, Celeste (trans.). White Pine Press

Kramer, Aaron, et al. (ed.). Cross-Cultural Communications

Kramer, Chuck (ed.). *Step into the Light— Poems from Recovery*. Great Lakes Poetry Press

Kroll, Judith. *Our Elephant & That Child*. The Quarterly Review of Literature Poetry Series

Kumin, Maxine. *Looking for Luck*. W.W Norton

Kyger, Joanne. *Just Space: Poems 1979-1989*. Black Sparrow Press

L

Lagomarsino, Nancy. *The Secretary Parables*. alicejamesbooks

Lai, Him Mark, et al. (trans.). *Island: Poetry and History of Chinese Immigrants on Angel Island, 1910-40*. University of Washington Press

Lane, Helen (trans.). Harcourt, Brace

Lane, Pinkie Gordon. *Girl at the Window*. Louisiana State University Press

Lane, W. C. *The Passing Thought of a Country Man*. Brunswick Publishing Corporation

Langille, Carole Glasser. *All That Glitters in Water*. New Poets Series/ Chestnut Hills Press

Langland, Joseph. *Selected Poems*. University of Massachusetts Press

Lappin, Kendall (trans.). *Gallic Echoes: A Selection of Poems*. Asylum Arts
——— (trans.). Asylum Arts

Laughlin, J., et al. (ed.). *New Directions in Prose and Poetry 55*. New Directions

Lawrence, D. H. *Birds, Beasts and Flowers!* Black Sparrow Press

Lawrence, Patricia A. *In the Wind's Eye*. Poetic Page

Lazer, Hank. *Doublespace: Poems 1971-1989*. Segue Books
———. *Inter(ir)ruptions*. Generator Press

Lea, Sydney. *The Blainville Testament*. Story Line Press

Leer, Norman. *I Dream My Father in a Song*. Mellen Poetry Press

Lehman, David. *The Line Forms Here*. University of Michigan Press

LeMaster, J. R. *Journey to Beijing*. Mellen Poetry Press

M

R

Rutsala, Vern. *Selected Poems*. Story Line Press

S

Sagan, Miriam. *True Body*. Parallax Press

Saigyo. *Poems of a Mountain Home*. Columbia University Press

Saint, Assoto (ed.). *Here to Dare*. Galiens Press
——— (ed.). *The Road Before Us: 100 Gay Black Poets*. Galiens Press

Salinas, Luis Omar. *Follower of Dusk*. Flume Press

Samaras, Nicholas. *Hands of the Saddlemaker*. Yale University Press

Sampson, Dennis. *Forgiveness*. Milkweed Editions

Sampson, Mary York. *52 Sonnets*. The Bank Street Press

Sánchez, Elba Rosario. *Tallos de luna/Moon Shoots*. Moving Parts Press

Sanchez, Jr., Trinidad. *Why Am I So Brown?* MARCH/Abrazo Press

Savageau, Cheryl. *Home Country*. alicejamesbooks

Scammacca, Nat, et al. (trans.). Cross-Cultural Communications

Schimmel, Annemarie (trans.). Shambhala Publications

Schmidt, Jan Zlotnik. *We Speak in Tongues*. Mellen Poetry Press

Schneeman, Elio. *Along the Rails*. United Artists Books

Schofield, Don. *Of Dust*. March Street Press

Schwartz, Alvin. *And the Green Grass Grew All Around: Folk Poetry from Everyone*. HarperCollins/Children's Division

Schwartz, Leonard. *Gnostic Blessing*. Goats + Compasses

Seager, Steven A. *Thirteenth at Love's Table*. American Literary Press

Seaton, Maureen. *The Sea Among the Cupboards*. New Rivers Press

Seay, James. *The Light As They Found It*. William Morrow

Seiferle, Rebecca (trans.). Sheep Meadow Press

Selby, Spencer. *House of Before*. Potes & Poets
———. *Stigma*. Score Publications

Seng-ts'an. *Hsin-hsin-ming*. Generator Press

Senghor, Léopold Sédar. *The Collected Poetry*. University Press of Virginia

Sevillano, Mando. *The Loneliness of Old Men: Anthropoems*. Eagle Publishing

Shaddock, David. *In This Place Where SOMETHING'S MISSING Lives*. Alileah Press

Shakespeare, William. *The Essential Shakespeare*. The Ecco Press

Shange, Ntozake. *A Daughter's Geography*. St. Martin's Press

INDEX BY TITLE

M

N

Oma's Story. Gina Bergamino. Ancient Mariners Press

Omeros. Derek Walcott. Farrar, Straus and Giroux/Noonday

On the Air with Dylan Thomas: The Broadcasts. Dylan Thomas. New Directions

One Tough Mother. John A. Todras. New Press Chapbooks

One-Hundred Butterflies. Peter Levitt. Broken Moon Press

Only Companion: Japanese Poems of Love and Longing. Sam Hamill (trans.). Shambhala Publications

Only the Raw Hands Are Heaven. Naomi Thiers. Washington Writers' Publishing House

Open Drawer, The. Rufus Goodwin. Urban Press

Open Season. Gina Bergamino. Ancient Mariners Press

Ordinary Messengers. Michael Hannon. Floating Island Publications

Other Dancers. Justin Spring. March Street Press

Other Hemisphere, The. Jan Kemp. Three Continents Press

Other Voice: Essays on Modern Poetry, The. Octavio Paz. Harcourt, Brace

Our Elephant & That Child. Judith Kroll. The Quarterly Review of Literature Poetry Series

Our Nuclear Heritage. James Sherry. Sun & Moon Press

Out of Bounds. Harry Mathews. Burning Deck

Out of Canaan. Mary Stewart Hammond. W.W. Norton

Out of Silence: Selected Poems. Muriel Rukeyser. TriQuarterly Books

Out of the Labyrinth: Selected Poems. Charles Henri Ford. City Lights Books

Out of This World: An Anthology of the St. Mark's Poetry Project, 1966-1991. Anne Waldman (ed.). Crown Publishers

Outer Life: The Poetry of Brendan Galvin. Brendan Galvin. Ampersand Press

Outside History. Eavan Boland. W.W. Norton

Ovid's Heroines: A Verse Translation of the Heroides. Daryl Hine (trans.). Yale University Press

Oxota: A Short Russian Novel. Lyn Hejinian. The Figures

P

Parallel to the Shore. Michael Melcher. Runaway Spoon Press

Park. Cole Swensen. Floating Island Publications

Passing Duration. Stephen Rodefer. Burning Deck

Passing Thought of a Country Man, The. W. C. Lane. Brunswick Publishing Corporation

Passion of Creation. Adams. Cypress House Press

Passionate Distance, A. Joan Gartland. Ridgeway Press

To See. Michael McFee. North Carolina Wesleyan College Press

To the Left of the Worshiper. Jeffrey Greene. alicejamesbooks

To Urania. Joseph Brodsky. Farrar, Straus and Giroux/Noonday

To Woo & To Wed: Poets on Love & Marriage. Michael Blumenthal (ed.). Poseidon Press

Tongue Bearer's Daughter, The. Jake Berry. Luna Bisonte Prods

Town House Gardens. Victoria Parsons Pennoyer. Parsons Field Press

Towns Facing Railroads. Jo McDougall. University of Arkansas Press

Traces. Aaron Rosen. Sheep Meadow Press

Trilce. César Vallejo. Sheep Meadow Press. Also Marsilio Publishers

Trimmings. Harryette Mullen. Tender Buttons

True Body. Miriam Sagan. Parallax Press

Truth and Lies That Press for Life: 60 Los Angeles Poets. Connie Hershey (ed.). Artifact Press

Truth, War, and the Dream-Game. Lawrence Fixel. Coffee House Press

Turbulence. Pierre Joris. St. Lazaire Press

Twelve Parts of Her. Jena Osman. Burning Deck

Twenties: 100 Poems. Jackson Mac Low. Roof Books

24-7-365. Reginald Elliott Gaines. The Poet Tree/New Spirit/I.O.T.A.

Two. Stan Cohen. Steam Press - Lad Publishing

Typing in the Dark. Saundra Sharp. Harlem River Press

U

U.S. Latino Literature: An Essay and Annotated Bibliography. Marc Zimmerman. MARCH/Abrazo Press

uh oh. Karl Daegling. We Press

unclear family. Damian Lopes. Runaway Spoon Press

Uncollected Poems. Basil Bunting. Oxford University Press

Under a Cat's-Eye Moon. Martha M. Vertreace. Clockwatch Review Press

Under Flag. Myung Mi Kim. Kelsey St. Press

Under the Tongue. Larry Zirlin. Hanging Loose Press

underfoot. David C. Kopaska-Merkel. Runaway Spoon Press

Unending Dialogue: Voices from an AIDS Poetry Workshop. Rachel Hadas. Faber and Faber

Unknown Country, The. Jeff Oaks. State Street Press

Unravelling Words and the Weaving Water. Cecilia Vicuña. Graywolf Press

Untidy Bride, The. Sandra Nicholls. Quarry Press

Uplands Haunted By The Sea. Walt Franklin. Great Elm Press

127865

COLOPHON

The text was set in Times New Roman, a typeface that was commissioned by The Times in London and produced under the supervision of Stanley Morison.

The book was composed collaboratively by the staffs of Poets House and Asphodel Press and compiled through the Poets House Poetry Publication Showcase. The indexes were done by Alabama Book Composition, Deatsville, Alabama. The book was printed by The Haddon Craftsmen, Scranton, Pennsylvania, on acid free paper.